D1604985

Hoshin Handbook

Third Edition

Chart the course for your organization

Pete Babich

Total Quality
Engineering

Copyright © 2005 Pete Babich

All rights reserved. No part of this publication may be reproduced, stored in a retrieval system or transmitted in any form or by any means electronic, mechanical, photocopying, recording or otherwise, without the prior written permission of the publisher.

Published by:
Total Quality Engineering, Inc.
15997 Grey Stone Rd, Poway CA 92064, USA

Printed in the United States of America; June, 2007.

Library of Congress Control Number: 2005911263
ISBN: 0-9651861-2-1

To order additional copies of the Hoshin Handbook, Third Edition contact:

    Total Quality Engineering, Inc.
    15997 Grey Stone Rd
    Poway CA 92064 USA
    +1-858-748-2916
    tqeinfo@tqe.com   http://www.tqe.com

Table of Contents

Preface

I was first introduced to the concepts of Hoshin Planning in 1986. I was intrigued by Hoshin and felt it could solve many of the planning problems I was experiencing as the quality manager for the San Diego Division of Hewlett-Packard. I facilitated the implementation of Hoshin within the division and became a student of the process. It was not long before I became the resident expert on Hoshin Planning and constantly fielded questions regarding the correct use of the forms or the underlying intent. I answered the questions, but I did not have a document to give them so they could answer their own questions.

Today, there are a number of books available that address the subject of *Hoshin Kanri* directly or discuss it using the term *Policy Deployment*. I have listed many of these sources in the bibliography. Although these references do a very good job of defining the intent and philosophy of Hoshin, they do not provide the reader with specific steps necessary for successful implementation. I found that new Hoshin users tend to ask basic questions like, "Which forms do I use" or "What information goes in this block?" New users wanted a step by step process to guide them.

Unfortunately, Hoshin is implemented in many different ways. Since there is no one correct way to implement Hoshin, it's difficult to provide step-by-step instructions unless a specific form of Hoshin is defined. This handbook is intended to be a "how to" book for a form of Hoshin that I have found effective and compatible with the culture in my organization. It defines a specific set of Hoshin forms and rules for their use. In addition, it attempts to provide background and insight so the forms and rules can be adapted to other situations.

I left Hewlett-Packard in 1991 to form my own business, and one of the first products I created was the *Hoshin Handbook*. The irony is that while I was employed by Hewlett-Packard, I never had time to create such a document. Although I used publicly available reference sources to research some of the historical elements of Hoshin, the bulk of the handbook is the result of my own personal experience. It describes the processes and

best practices that I have found to be most useful. The *Hoshin Handbook* is used as the text in my Hoshin Workshops and was the guide for development of Hoshin software. The software addresses one of the biggest barriers to Hoshin implementation: too much paperwork!

The *Hoshin Handbook, Third Edition* builds upon the original *Hoshin Handbook* that was published in 1992 and the *Hoshin Handbook, Second Edition* published in 1996. Each chapter has been expanded to include more detailed discussions of concepts, principles, and examples. The third edition includes a CD with lectures and worksheets on each subject so that it can function as a self-study guide. A Hoshin Workshop Leader's Guide can be purchased separately to make training everyone on the concepts of Hoshin as easy as possible.

I'm very encouraged by the reception of the Hoshin process. Twenty years ago if I asked someone if they had ever heard of Hoshin, the response would have been, "Huh?" Today, many people have heard of it and are intrigued by its potential. Be warned, however, Hoshin is not a "silver bullet." It's just one element of a complete Total Quality Management system. It can, however, play an important role to improve the effectiveness of any organization that takes the time to use it correctly.

I believe the *Hoshin Handbook Third Edition* provides new users with the tools necessary to begin their own Hoshin implementation. Using TQE's Hoshin software is a way to truly make the organization's Hoshin plan a living, evolving document. This handbook would have been very beneficial to me during my own Hoshin implementation. I hope it provides you with the inspiration and tools to improve your organization's planning process by implementing Hoshin Kanri.

In conclusion, I would like to thank my customers for their feedback and suggestions for improvement and my sons Pete and John for their help. I wish you luck with your Hoshin implementation, and may all your plans be realized.

Pete Babich

 Total Quality Engineering

Chapter 1

A Personal History

The first time I heard the word "Hoshin" was early in 1986. I was the engineering assurance manager of the San Diego Division of Hewlett-Packard. My boss, the division quality manager, was complaining about having to attend an organization wide quality manager's meeting. He was upset because he felt that little was ever accomplished during the meetings. "All they ever talk about is that damn Hoshin," he exclaimed. "It's nothing more than a paperwork jungle and we just don't need it." Well needless to say, my first impression of Hoshin was not very good.

As it turned out, my boss retired from HP, and I was promoted to the position of division quality manager. I ended up attending the meeting that he was complaining about. It was an annual gathering of all Hewlett-Packard quality managers. The theme of the four-day meeting was devoted entirely to Hoshin.

Since I was a new quality manager, I didn't know most of the other managers attending the meeting. As I met them, I asked about their experience with Hoshin. The response I got was significantly different from what I expected. Many said they had just started using Hoshin during the last year and that it was really great. It had become a key part of their business success. I was surprised at how pervasive that view was. I had great respect for my previous boss; but based on the apparent overwhelming approval of Hoshin, I was beginning to conclude that he misjudged the process.

The sessions began with numerous testimonials about how great Hoshin was. There was a panel of general managers. Each said they had implemented Hoshin in their divisions and they were really glad they did. Considering the rave reviews, my curiosity was highly peaked, but I still had no idea what Hoshin really was.

It was late in the first day before I got my first glimpse of the Hoshin process. We were separated into small teams and began to review a case study that was designed to illustrate the concepts of Hoshin. The first part of the case study described the situation of a division in trouble. Orders were down and the division seemed to lack focus. The quality manager, who just happened to have recently attended a class on Hoshin, seized the opportunity to introduce his general manager to Hoshin Planning. As the case study progressed, the highly insightful quality manager coached and supported his boss as they crafted a Hoshin plan to turn the division around.

At this point, I became skeptical. To me, the case study seemed like so much fluff and appeared to be focused more on psychology than planning management. I questioned our group's facilitator to learn more about the mechanics of the process. His answers were vague and evasive. I was not convinced he knew anything about Hoshin. I was frustrated and began to appreciate my ex-boss's concerns. Luckily, I was sitting next to the quality manager from Singapore. Seeing my frustration, he leaned over and whispered, "Don't believe all this stuff. Hoshin is a great tool, but it's not going to save the world."

Later that evening, I made sure that I sat next to him at dinner. I learned that much of the concepts being presented were piloted in Singapore. The case study seemed to be concentrating on the concept of breakthrough objectives and deploying them through the organization. He stressed the importance of focusing on business fundamentals first. He also scoffed at managers proclaiming the virtues of Hoshin when they had used it for less than one year. In his opinion, because of the potential for complexity and confusion, real gain does not occur for at least three years.

As the session continued, we were gradually exposed to the mechanics of Hoshin. I began to understand the power it could have. The typical HP culture was Management by Objectives (MBO), that is, provide employees with broad objectives and let them figure how to accomplish the objectives on their own. Management did not give direction. Instead, employees were encouraged to use their creative talents to find ways to accomplish the objectives. The intent was to empower employees and rely on their creativity to achieve breakthroughs. Obviously, HP had been successful with this style. As an engineer, I related very well to MBO, but as a manager, I was also aware of its pitfalls.

Objectives were typically set annually at the corporate, group, and division level. They were rarely set at section or department level. The annual objectives consisted of ten to fifteen things we wanted improve throughout the year. The objectives were also very broad and general. I viewed them as never ending, God, country, and apple pie type objectives. Examples were "Improve time to market", "Make TQC a way of life", and "Improve product quality". Because the objectives were loosely defined and rarely reviewed, progress was spotty. There were many examples of someone achieving great success with respect to one or more objectives; but for the most part, progress was small

Total Quality Engineering

and uncoordinated. Since there was always room for more improvement, the old objectives were trotted out year after year with little or no change.

In addition, the MBO annual objectives did not address the things we did day to day. They also did not place any priority on activities. For example, would it be OK to let shipments slip so we could staff a project to improve time to market? Of course, the unwritten rules had an answer for this question, but there was nothing in the MBO structure to address this situation. Objectives were also misused to justify pet projects of individuals. If one could somehow link their project to an annual objective, then it had significance. People disagreeing with the project ran the risk of having to defend why they did not believe the annual objective was a good thing. Of course, there was little discussion regarding how this project would actually support the annual objective and even less discussion as to whether the project was the best strategy to achieve the annual objective.

This lack of structure allowed people to run off in many different directions, all in the name of some annual objective. Sometimes one group would pick an objective and another group would pick a different objective, and their efforts would be diametrically opposed to each other. The classic confrontation was between the R&D Manager and me. I had my people working on things to improve product reliability. A key strategy was to increase product testing. The R&D Manager viewed those efforts as hampering his ability to decrease product time to market.

What I liked about Hoshin was that it provided structure to address the shortcoming of MBO. It separated the day to day activities from the breakthrough activities. It focused breakthrough efforts on a few specific things instead of broad generalities. It provided a method to coordinate activities of multiple functions and areas. I also recognized that implementation would not be a "slam-dunk." MBO had been around for many years, and most people felt little need to change. The Corporate Quality Manager also appreciated that concern. In his closing remarks, he did not attack MBO. Instead, he attempted to adapt Hoshin to MBO by referring to Hoshin as Turbo-MBO. As a going away gift, we all received a T-shirt with a Turbo-MBO logo. I left the meeting convinced that Hoshin was a tool that could help my division become more competitive. I was ready to change the planning process at San Diego Division.

Wearing my new T-shirt, I attended the next San Diego Division staff meeting. I excitedly shared my newfound knowledge and was shocked to learn how much my peers were opposed to Hoshin. I was almost physically thrown out of the room! They expressed concern that it was too much work, had no benefit, and would hamper creativity. Recognizing the need for self-preservation, I quickly backed off my push to implement Hoshin at the division. I pointed out that I still felt Hoshin was valuable, and that I would pilot it within the quality function first.

Licking my wounds, I announced to my staff that I planned to begin using Hoshin. Their response was much the same as division staff, except it was not as vocal. Since I was their boss, opposition was not as forceful, but they sure were not happy about being the guinea pigs either. It was obvious that implementing this change was not going to be easy. We began by jumping right into creating annual objectives using the Hoshin format. Old habits die hard, as our session produced a list of eight broad scope objectives, many of which were really just improvements of ongoing activities. The exercise did not produce a clear unifying plan. It only added a lot of complication and paperwork to what had been a simple process. My staff was quick to point this out to me and suggested we scrap the whole process.

The objectives we came up with were a mishmash of business basics and true breakthrough thinking. We tried to make the annual plan cover all bases. I remembered the Singapore manager's comments that stressed a focus on business fundamentals first. I told my staff that I agreed with their assessment of how poorly we had done on our first attempt at developing a Hoshin Plan. I then suggested that maybe we started too fast and needed to focus on the fundamentals first.

It was now even clearer to me that I needed to proceed slowly. I was changing culture, and that is always difficult. I decided a step-by-step approach would be best. I first established a process of conducting a monthly department review with each manager. I then set an expectation for the managers to present a statement of their department's mission at their first meeting. They were to work with their staff to get consensus on their mission statements.

As it turned out, that move proved very beneficial. Forcing my staff to meet with their staff and discuss their mission provided for some lively discussion. Many of my managers were surprised at how differently people in the same department perceived their mission. The discussion brought department personnel closer by collectively developing a clearer understanding of their expectations. When the missions were presented at the meeting, I had difficulty with some of them. The ensuing discussions changed either my opinion or their mission statements. We ended with everyone having a clearer understanding of what was expected and how each department contributed to the success of the quality function and the division.

My next step was to ask each manager, "How do you know your department is doing a good job?" At the next meeting, they were expected to present a list of at least four things they would measure to evaluate their department's performance. The only criterion was that any measure chosen had to be represented in graphical form. They were not required to show any data. They just had to identify the measures. At the meeting, most people showed up with four measures. One manager had only one measure and argued it was all he needed. I explained to him that he needed to find three more measures. Another manager had ten measures. One of which was the "number of rings before the phone was answered." To him I said, "Very well."

I delayed the next meeting for two months to allow for data collection. At the meeting, each manager presented the graphs of their data. Over half of the measures had changed. During the data collection process, they learned that some measures did not yield insight into process performance or were extremely difficult to collect. As a result, they changed many of the measures. The manager that said he was going to measure ten items showed up with only four graphs. He commented that many of the measures were redundant and problems in one area would typically show up in other measures. The measure of "number of rings..." was scrapped because of the difficulty of collecting the data. He selected instead the "number of outside caller abandonments," which could easily be determined from the telephone monthly report.

The manager that said he only needed one measure showed up with four. He became a strong advocate for the need of counter balancing performance measures. For example, if you only had a measure of "product shipments," it could be achieved by shipping bad units. By adding the counter balancing measure of "number of rejects," optimizing one measure at the expense of another is eliminated.

One manager also shared how collecting the data could be made relatively painless. He had selected "equipment utilization hours" as one of his measures. The only way he could collect the data was to create equipment usage logs and record the number of hours each piece of equipment was operated. This was very time consuming. The manager explained that a department technician noticed that an environmental chamber had a meter on it that displayed the hours of operation. The technician suggested putting similar meters on all equipment. The meters were installed, and the data collection process was reduced to a ten-minute task once a week. In addition, you did not have to worry about someone forgetting to enter usage hours into a log.

The process of getting our business fundamentals under control took almost nine months. Everyone believed it had been a valuable process. Each manager and employee had clear understanding of their job expectations and very good measures of performance. I also had confidence everyone was working on the "right things." This allowed me to shift most of the day-to-day management to my managers and their staff. I was free to devote more time to breakthrough issues.

With business fundamentals running on automatic, we then began the process of setting annual breakthrough objectives. This time it went much more smoothly. The process was not cluttered with business fundamentals, and we very quickly settled on supporting the HP 10X reliability improvement as our only breakthrough objective. This objective was carefully deployed to all departments with direct impact. Departments that did not have direct impact were free to choose breakthrough objectives that related to their specific issues. The process went very smoothly, and subsequent monthly reviews showed we met our plan exactly.

I shared my success with division staff management, and they agreed to try the concepts at their level. One year after my introduction to Hoshin, the San Diego Division developed a Hoshin plan that was deployed only to division senior managers. This means that only seven people had any knowledge of the plan. At the time, the division employed over 1,400 people. Our plan had eight key strategies. Throughout the year we reviewed our progress and experienced most of the same problems my function had experienced. We debated whether a strategy should be part of business fundamentals or breakthrough objectives. We debated the value of certain performance measures. The debate, however, was positive as it helped everyone gain understanding into the Hoshin process. Probably the most important thing learned was that Hoshin did not suppress creativity. In fact, it helped focus creativity to solve problems. The plan creation and review process allowed many opportunities for creative, innovative ideas to influence our strategies and action plan. In addition, senior management learned that the paperwork was not overwhelming, and it provided a valuable structure to organize and rationalize ideas.

The next year, we created a Division Annual Hoshin Plan that had only five key strategies. It was deployed to section manager level. We were now involving more people, which had the potential for creating more process related questions than I could answer. As luck would have it, senior management decided to have all managers attend a new class called the Process of Management (POM). This class was five days long with the third day devoted entirely to planning. The original POM training material created by corporate acknowledged that HP used many different types of planning processes. It noted that Hoshin existed, but the lecture material was generic in nature. I decided to become a POM instructor, and I modified the planning section to teach the concepts of Hoshin. As a result, I was able to teach Hoshin to all managers and supervisors on the site within a one year period. It provided just-in-time training as we deployed Hoshin to the full site.

By the following year, we were becoming pretty proficient with Hoshin planning. We had integrated the Hoshin process with our annual product planning process. Key strategies had been reduced to three, and we were getting much better at critically analyzing our progress and making mid-course corrections. We were consistently meeting our objectives and setting even more challenging ones. During a corporate TQM review, we were judged to have one of the best planning processes in the corporation.

Implementing Hoshin was not easy. It was a lot of hard work. Many cultural barriers had to be overcome. It required learning a new value of supporting all decisions with data, but it allowed us to make better decisions. By focusing the Division's efforts on a few key objectives, we achieved much more progress than when we simply hoped things would get better by themselves. I am convinced that Hoshin played a major role in establishing the San Diego Division of Hewlett-Packard as a world class supplier of graphic plotters and color printers.

I left Hewlett-Packard in 1991 to form my own business, and I have continued to use Hoshin in my new business. Startup companies tend to go in many directions at once. My own entrepreneurial efforts have been no different. Each day brings a new unexpected challenge or opportunity. My Hoshin plan has been a stabilizing force. During each monthly review, I evaluate each activity to see if it's in concert with the plan. Sometimes it's not consistent with the plan, and I adjust priorities and activities appropriately. My Hoshin plan allows me to "keep my eye on the goal."

In conclusion, I have learned that Hoshin is not a "silver bullet." It's just one element of a complete Total Quality Management system. In addition, being proficient with the Hoshin process takes work. You can't become a world-class athlete by reading books and watching other people play. You must get into the game and practice, practice, practice. Hoshin is no different. You must start using the process and continually fine tune it to meet your needs. If you take the time to use it correctly, Hoshin can play an important role to improve the effectiveness of your organization.

Chapter 2

Hoshin Overview

Planning as an Integral Part of Organization Management

Most people would agree that an effective planning process is critical to long term organization success. To be effective, however, planning must be integrated into the overall management process. If there was one magic recipe for success, everyone would be using it and there would be no need for a book like this. Unfortunately, success depends on an infinite number of variables, many of which are uncontrollable. In spite of the complexities, some organizations consistently perform well. They have consistent growth, loyal customers, proud employees and attractive profits. Examples of such organizations are 3M, AT&T, Boeing, IBM, Los Alamos National Bank, Motorola, Pearl River School District, Ritz-Carlton, Solectron, Texas Nameplate, and Xerox[1].

No two organizations manage exactly the same way, but excellent organizations tend to do similar things in key, important areas. A popular title that describes this collective set of behaviors is Total Quality Management or TQM. In the US we are fortunate to have an excellent model of TQM. It's the Malcolm Baldrige National Quality Award (MBNQA). The award criteria were developed by studying the traits and behaviors of excellent organizations, and it's continually being modified to reflect changes in those traits and behaviors. The primary purpose of the MBNQA is to be a **standard of excellence** that will help US organizations achieve world-class status. The award criteria has three important roles in strengthening US competitiveness: 1) help improve organizational performance practices, capabilities, and results, 2) facilitate communication and sharing of best practices among US organizations of all types, and 3) serve as a working tool for understanding and managing performance and for guiding

---

[1] All of these organizations are Malcolm Baldrige National Quality Award winners. Most winners have consistently out performed market averages but a few have fallen on hard times. Over the long term, however, I will invest my money in organizations like Baldrige winners.

organizational planning and opportunities for learning. The first awards were presented in 1988. Through 2005, there have been fifty-nine winners and all represent organizational excellence in their fields.

Japan has a similar model of TQM called the Deming Application Prize. The first Deming Prize was awarded in 1951. The Union of Japanese Scientists and Engineers (JUSE) manages the award and is instrumental in sharing best practices with the Japanese industry. Organizations like Cannon, Matsushita, Sony, and Toyota have used those best practices to achieve world-class results.

Table 1 shows the main categories of the two TQM models. Table 2 lists some of the sub-categories that relate specifically to planning. Neither model is a recipe for success, but I don't know of any better models. If organizations implemented these models, I believe they would have a better chance of achieving organizational excellence.

Table 1: TQM Categories

MBNQA[2]	Deming Prize[3]
1. Leadership. 2. Strategic Planning. 3. Customer and Market Focus. 4. Measurement, Analysis, and Knowledge Management. 5. Human Resource Focus. 6. Process Management. 7. Business Results.	1. Policy and objectives. 2. Organization and its operation. 3. Education and its dissemination. 4. Assembling and disseminating information and its utilization. 5. Analysis. 6. Standardization. 7. Control. 8. Quality assurance. 9. Effects. 10. Future Plans.

Table 2: Characteristics of Planning

MBNQA	Deming Prize
1. Focus on customer satisfaction and operational capability. 2. Align daily work with strategic directions. 3. Include mechanism to transmit requirements and achieve alignment. 4. Define clear and measurable performance objectives. 5. Evaluate progress relative to expectations and competitors.	1. Identify quality policy. 2. Align objectives with quality policy. 3. Deploy objectives throughout organization. 4. Define relationship between long-range and short-range plans. 5. Identify clear-cut lines of responsibility. 6. Check objectives and their implementation.

---

[2] Source: Baldrige National Quality Program, 2005 Criteria for Performance Excellence.
[3] Source: "What is Total Quality Control" by Kaoru Ishikawa.

 Total Quality Engineering

 Hoshin

The planning process helps focus activity on the key things necessary for success. Peter Drucker[4] states that business planning is rooted in answering three basic business questions:

What *is* our business?
What *will* it be?
What *should* it be?

The planning process must define why the organization exists. That existence is not defined by products and services, but by customer needs. Because customer needs change over time, the planning process must also address why the organization will continue to exist in the future. In addition, the planning process must address the difficult choice of reacting to the future or influencing it.

Effective Planning Techniques

By studying TQM models like the MBNQA and the Deming Prize and books by Drucker and other experts, you will observe many common themes. Listed below are attributes of effective planning techniques that I have developed from my own study and observations of world-class organizations:

Effective planning:
- is driven by an understanding of customer needs (present and future)
- balances daily management with strategic objectives
- identifies the critical few objectives
- evaluates resource constraints
- establishes performance measures
- develops detailed implementation plans
- identifies ownership and accountability
- conducts regular reviews of progress
- continually improves the process of planning

Given that this list identifies characteristics of effective planning, then if a planning process embodied these characteristics it would be a good choice to use. The intent of this handbook is to show that Hoshin Kanri implements effective planning techniques.

---

[4] Source: "The Practice of Management" by Peter F. Drucker.

History of Hoshin Kanri

Hoshin Kanri was developed in Japan. After World War II, Japan was faced with the difficult task of rebuilding just about everything. Japan had suffered a military defeat, and the Allied forces did not want Japan's military might to resurface. General Douglas MacArthur commanded the occupying forces. His objective was to help Japan rebuild its economy and infrastructure without allowing the military to be rebuilt.

MacArthur enlisted the resources of many American experts to help with the reconstruction. Homer Sarasohn, an engineer from MIT, headed the Civil Communication Section (CCS). In Japan's view, the US was still the enemy and was occupying their country. The responsibility of the CCS was to establish an information and education center to inform the Japanese populace that Americans did not mean to terrorize the Japanese. The method selected to accomplish that objective was radio communication. Unfortunately, no one had radios.

The CCS needed to establish manufacturing capacity to build radios. Production facilities and raw materials were scarce. Because wartime managers were prevented from positions of responsibility, the management teams were new and unskilled. Because scrap was high and reliability was low, the first radios built were anything but quality products. The National Electrical Testing Laboratory was established to "inspect in quality." This helped, but the CCS recognized it was not a long term solution. They adopted a strategy of training Japanese managers and engineers in management techniques. Statistical Quality Control (SQC) and the work of Walter Shewhart were included in the training.

The CCS worked with the Japanese Union of Scientists and Engineers (JUSE) to conduct the management training. JUSE was responsible for vocational and technical education. They also felt that SQC was a major reason the US won the war. JUSE wanted more training in SQC and asked the CCS to recommend an expert to continue their learning. Shewhart was the obvious choice, but he was unavailable. The next best choice was a professor at Columbia University that had studied and applied Shewhart's methods. Mr. Sarasohn recommended W. Edwards Deming.

Deming had made a previous visit to Japan in 1947 as part of an economic survey mission. Japanese and government officials were already familiar with him; therefore, JUSE asked Deming to provide the expert training. During a two-month period in June 1950, Deming trained hundreds of engineers, managers, and scholars. He also conducted a session for top management. Deming's lectures focused on three key areas: the use of the PDCA cycle, the importance of understanding the causes of variation, and process control through the use of control charts.

Through Deming's training and JUSE's subsequent training, Japan began a major effort to improve quality by implementing Statistical Quality Control. Initial results were

positive, but Japan entered a period of overemphasis on SQC. Engineers continued to push SQC, but workers resisted, data collection techniques were inadequate, and top management did not show much interest. In 1954, JUSE invited Joseph M. Juran to lecture on management's role in promoting quality control activities. Juran's visit marked a turning point in Japan's quality maturity. They shifted from primarily dealing with technology to an overall concern for total quality management.

Juran pointed out that it was management's responsibility to lead quality improvement efforts. A key element of that responsibility was to define the quality policy and assure that everyone understood and supported it. Management saw the organization's planning process as the vehicle for them to fulfill their responsibility for quality management. At about the same time as Juran's visit, Peter Drucker's book *The Practice of Management,* which described the concepts of Management by Objectives, was published in Japanese.

The Japanese blended Deming and Juran's teachings with the concepts of Management by Objectives and began their first attempts at strategic quality planning. Each organization created its own planning processes. The Deming Application Prize shared best planning practices, and common themes began to appear. In 1957, Kaoru Ishikawa published a paper stressing the importance of management and operational policies. Juran made another visit in 1960, emphasizing the responsibility of management for setting goals and planning for improvement.

Japanese planning techniques continued to evolve and improve. In 1965, Bridgestone Tire published a report analyzing the planning techniques used by Deming Prize winning companies. The techniques described were given the name *hoshin kanri.* By 1975, Hoshin was widely accepted in Japan.

Hoshin began to creep into the US in the early 80's. This occurred mainly because some US companies had divisions or subsidiaries in Japan that were Deming Prize winners. The winning companies include Hewlett-Packard's YHP Division, Fuji-Xerox, and Texas Instrument's Oita plant. Other US companies like Florida Power and Light searched for Japanese companies in their industry.

As a former employee of Hewlett-Packard, I can speak with some authority about the Hewlett-Packard experience. YHP is a division of Hewlett-Packard in Japan. In 1977, YHP's president, Kenzo Sasaoka, embarked on a journey to win the Deming Prize. YHP was awarded the Deming prize in 1982, after demonstrating impressive improvement in almost all elements of its business. Examples include increased productivity of 91%, decreased inventory of 64%, and increased profit of 177%. Mr. Sasaoka, like other Deming prize winners, attributed much of YHP's success to the use of *hoshin kanri.* As a result of YHP's success, it seemed that every Hewlett-Packard manager made pilgrimages to Japan. Hewlett-Packard Corporate Quality helped by standardizing the forms and training division quality managers. Hewlett-Packard considered Hoshin Kanri

as a competitive advantage, and until the early 1990s it was treated as "Company Private."

English Translation

Understanding the origin of the words can provide insight into Hoshin concepts. The term "Hoshin" is short for *hoshin kanri*. The word *hoshin* can be broken into two parts. The literal translation of *ho* is "direction." The literal translation of *shin* is "needle," so the word *hoshin* could translate into "direction needle" or the English equivalent of "compass." The word kanri can also be broken into two parts. The first part, *kan*, translates into control or channeling. The second part, *ri*, translates into reason or logic. Taken altogether, *hoshin kanri* means management and control of the organization's direction needle or focus.

ho = direction, side

shin = needle

hoshin = a course, a policy, a plan, an aim

kan = control, pipe, tube

理
ri = reason, logic, principle

kanri = administration, management, control, charge of, care for

The most popular English translation for Hoshin is "Policy Deployment." Many books by American authors use Policy Deployment as the name for Hoshin. No matter what you call it, however, Hoshin is effective and helps organizations become more competitive. For the rest of this handbook, I will refer to the process as Hoshin.

Management by Objectives (MBO)

As I mentioned before, Hoshin was developed by blending the elements of Management by Objectives (MBO) with the Plan-Do-Check-Act cycle. MBO was first documented in 1954 by Peter Drucker in his book *The Practice of Management*. If you haven't read this book, I strongly recommend it. It's still one of the best books on management that I have found.

The primary premise of MBO is that every organization must build a true team that works effectively together to achieve organization success. Each member of the team provides varying skills and contribution levels, but everyone must contribute toward a common goal. Their efforts must all pull in the same direction, without gaps, friction, or unnecessary duplication of effort. Drucker notes that organization effectiveness requires that each job be focused on organization objectives or goals. Individual results are measured by the contribution they make to the success of the whole organization.

Aligning the efforts of the organization is just the first part of MBO. To make MBO work, all effort must be measured in order for managers to have self-control. In other words, performance measurement provides managers with feedback regarding the health of the organization and allows them to make corrections.

A key concept of MBO is that when people have more control over their own work, they are more satisfied and productivity is increased. MBO was intended to provide managers with key objectives, resources, and the measures to control progress and then get out of their way. Given that everyone understands the organization objectives, individuals will use self-control to assure efforts are focused on achieving overall organization success.

One of the fundamental problems with MBO was that there was no defined process to use it. Drucker even went so far as to call MBO a "philosophy." This led many organizations to invent their own processes. Lots of "MBO" consultants entered the field using their own customized process and forms. On the whole, this effort was positive, but it also created many holes and problems.

Hewlett-Packard was an early adopter of MBO. It created a base MBO structure, but specific forms and processes were not defined. HP was so focused on individual freedom and creativity that many MBO efforts were never even reviewed. Since HP had multiple, broad scoped objectives, it was easy for people in different areas to address objectives with opposing results. Effort to assure all objectives were addressed was seldom performed. This resulted in a general lack of progress, and objectives were repeated year after year with little or no change.

It sounds like I am painting a bleak picture of HP's experience with MBO, but in reality MBO was a tremendous tool for HP. MBO helped pave the way for HP to expand from being a manufacturer of electronic measuring equipment to one of the largest computer

 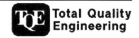

companies in the world. In spite of its success with MBO, however, HP ultimately shifted to using Hoshin as a way to improve its ability to execute its plans.

Japanese organizations adopting MBO also recognized its weaknesses. Since they had recently been exposed to systematic quality improvement concepts like PDCA from Deming and Juran, they ended up blending MBO with PDCA to create Hoshin Kanri.

Plan-Do-Check-Act (PDCA)

The Plan-Do-Check-Act (PDCA) cycle is often referred to as the Deming Cycle, because Deming introduced PDCA to Japan after World War II. However, the roots of PDCA were developed by Walter Shewhart; who is generally recognized at the father of Statistical Quality Control. Of all the tools used in quality improvement, the PDCA cycle is probably the most important. It describes the basic quality improvement process.

Simply put, the PDCA cycle is:

1. Plan what you want to accomplish and determine how you will know when it's accomplished.

2. Do what you planned; that is, work your plan.

3. Check how well your actual accomplishments compare to your expected accomplishments and analyze all deviations.

4. Act on all deviations from expected results by implementing immediate countermeasures. Standardize gains and reflect on what was learned.

5. Go to step 1.

The steps of the PDCA cycle are very simple, but people sometimes misuse it. Key components are slighted or missed altogether. Although Dr. Juran did not specifically cite the PDCA cycle in his *Quality Control Handbook*, he does describe an improvement cycle with seven steps. Dr. Ishikawa, in his book *What is Quality Control*, divided the PDCA cycle into six parts. Based on these subdivisions and my own experience, I have broken the PDCA cycle into the basic steps shown on the following page.

Plan-Do-Check-Act

4.1 Resolve immediate issues
4.2 Document and standardize all
   gains
4.3 Conduct training on all new
   processes
4.4 Reflect on lessons learned
4.5 Go to step 1.1
	1.1 Examine present status
	1.2 Identify improvement areas
	1.3 Establish performance measures
	   and goals
	1.4 Understand root cause of
	   current performance
	   1.5 Identify solution
	      alternatives
	   1.6 Select and schedule
	      solution

3.1 Compare actual results to
   expected results
3.2 Understand root cause of
   all deviations
	2.1 Conduct training on new
	   solution
	2.2 Implement scheduled action

A P C D

One of the most important aspects of PDCA is its "closed-loop" nature. The cycle is continually planning, evaluating results, and refining activity. This creates "cycles of learning" that can effectively allow plans to self-correct. For example, if a plan is completely wrong for a desired objective, the Check phase will expose that fact and the Action phase with adjust activity so it will be more in line with the objective. US organizations are generally very good at PD, but they often fail badly when it comes to CA. In my opinion, lack of effective CA is why many organizations are always in "firefight" mode.

Early Japanese MBO implementers used the closed loop nature of PDCA to modify MBO and create an improved planning structure. The structure was rooted in the philosophy of MBO, but it also included the rigor, data analysis, and cycles of learning of PDCA. The result was called Hoshin Kanri. As I describe Hoshin in the remainder of this handbook, you will see the essence of MBO and PDCA in every element of Hoshin Kanri.

So Just What Is Hoshin?

Hoshin is a system of *forms and rules* that provide structure for the planning process. It encourages people to analyze situations, create plans for improvement, conduct performance checks, and take appropriate action. It's a methodology driven by data and supported by documentation. Hoshin focuses the organization's efforts on the critical few things necessary for success.

There are five elements of a complete Hoshin Plan:

- The **Business Fundamentals Plan** documents daily work. Based on the organization's mission, it describes what the business *is*.

- The **Long Range Plan** documents how the organization expects to operate in the future. Based on the organization's vision, it describes what the business *should be*.

- The **Annual Plan** documents the key objectives that must be accomplished this year in order for the organization to move along the path toward achieving its long range plan and vision. It documents what the business *will be*.

- **Review Tables** compare actual results to expected results and document changes to the plan. Review Tables allow the plan to become a living document.

- **Abnormality Tables** document "out of the ordinary" occurrences and facilitate problem root cause removal.

Hoshin uses forms to facilitate the plan's documentation and execution. No two organizations use exactly the same set of forms, but the underlying intent of Hoshin Kanri is always retained. Chapter 7 describes a set of forms that I have found useful. The forms and processes described in this handbook should be viewed as one example. They can be modified as required to fit your organization's culture.

The following chapters will describe each element of the Hoshin plan in more detail.

Chapter 3

Mission and Key Activities

What is my job and how does it support the organization?

Two Aspects of Planning

Peter Drucker points out that managers must be concerned with two aspects of the organization. First, they must assure the organization is healthy today. Second, they must assure the organization will remain healthy in the future. Focusing on only one aspect rarely assures success. If you spend all of your resources focused on short-term returns, you will probably not be prepared to address the needs of customers in the future. If you spend all of your

Hoshin

Two Parts

1. Business Fundamentals (daily management)

2. Breakthrough Plans (change management)

X X X
X X X
X X X

resources focused on changing things to meet future needs, you will probably not have enough money to finance your efforts (unless you have a really big bank account). Both aspects of the organization must be managed effectively. Hoshin supports this philosophy by separating the organization's plan into two parts: business fundamentals and breakthroughs.

Business fundamentals are based on the organization's mission and document daily work. X x x After completing the Hoshin business fundamentals plan, everyone in the organization should understand how their efforts contribute to the organization's current performance. Breakthroughs are changes the organization must make so it can remain viable in the X X X future. Breakthroughs are based on the organization's vision and document key X X X improvement or change activity. Breakthroughs are further divided into Long Range and X X X annual plans. After completing breakthrough plans, everyone understands what they

must do to change the way the organization will operate in the future. Business fundamentals can be thought of as "keeping the ship afloat," while breakthroughs allow the organization to "explore uncharted lands."

Normally, most of each workday is devoted to business fundamentals. Workload staffing, however, should not require 100% of the organization's resources be devoted to business fundamentals. At least 10% to 20% of resources should be devoted to breakthrough activities. If the organization focuses only on business fundamentals, it may find that the world will pass it by. Business fundamentals do have the highest priority, however. If they are not performing to expectations, efforts focused on breakthroughs should be diverted until the business fundamentals are back in control. You can't pay your bills with promises of future performance!

Create the Mission Statement

The Hoshin business fundamentals plan is based on the mission of the organization. The mission is sometimes referred to as purpose, charter or business intent. It basically describes why the organization exists. It typically identifies customers and the fundamental customer needs the organization is fulfilling. Missions are appropriate at the organization level and at every operational unit within the organization. All lower level missions should link to the organization mission. When people understand why they are doing things and how it supports the whole organization, they are more motivated and can act independently and creatively to fulfill the mission.

Effective missions focus on markets and customers, not products and services. They tend to be specific, achievable, and motivating. Above all, effective missions are memorable. That is, people are able to recite their own mission and the organization's mission without having to refer to the back of a business card or a plaque hung on the wall in the lobby. Many missions are not memorable because they fill up a whole page with qualifiers and superlatives describing how the mission will be accomplished. These verbose missions are usually the result of a management off-site meeting where the managers tried to capture everything they want or ever will want in a statement that didn't offend anyone. The intent is noble, but the result is typically unusable. If people can't remember the mission, they will not integrate it into their daily decision making. Unless the mission is used on a daily basis to test the appropriateness of current and proposed activity, the effort to create the mission was wasted.

To develop a mission statement, it's important to answer some basic questions:

- Who are our customers?
- What are their needs?
- How will they measure our performance?
- What are our products and services?
- How well do our products and services satisfy customer needs?

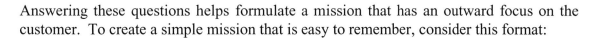

Answering these questions helps formulate a mission that has an outward focus on the customer. To create a simple mission that is easy to remember, consider this format:

"*To* satisfy the needs *of* some customers *by* providing, serving ..."

The mission does not have to address the needs of all customers. Of course you will serve all customers, but the Pareto[5] principle should be considered. Usually, there are just a few customers that will have a significant influence on what you do. It's their needs that will determine what kind of products and services you provide. Avoid complicating the mission by adding qualifiers, values, measures, and other "God, country and apple pie" statements. Values and measures are important and will be addressed in the next chapter, but it's best to keep them out of the mission. Keep the mission simple, so people can remember it! Consider the two mission alternatives of a fictitious utilities organization listed below:

> Our mission is to provide quality, responsive, and cost effective electrical power services to our diverse customer base through an innovative, talented, and dedicated work-force that believes in teamwork, good citizenship, fairness, integrity and is constantly striving for excellence in everything we do. We strive for the highest levels of customer satisfaction and work to provide our shareholders with acceptable returns.

> Improve the standard of living for Southern California commercial and residential customers by providing uninterrupted electrical power.

Which of the two missions is more likely to be remembered? Which one provides an outward focus on the customer? Which statement clearly identifies who and what is important? The secret to effective missions is to keep them simple and focused on how the customer will benefit from your products and services.

A key point in Hoshin Kanri is that business fundamentals document what the organization does today to serve today's customers. That means most missions will not include verbs that imply change. If the mission includes verbs like improve, reduce,

---

[5] A term popularized by Juran. It describes the process of separating the "vital few" from the "less important many". For more information: "Quality Control Handbook, Third Edition" by Joseph M. Juran.

implement, or establish it might imply that the mission describes something the organization doesn't currently do but wants to do in the future. In general, missions use verbs like manage, maintain, deliver, or serve. These verbs imply something the organization is currently doing. This is not a hard rule, but unless a change verb is focused on the customer, the mission might just be wishful thinking.

Deploy the Mission

After the organization's mission is created, it should be deployed to every operational unit within the organization. Mission deployment can be described as dividing the mission into lower level activities essential to achieving the mission. Missions are generally deployed along organizational lines. When helping organizations implement Hoshin, one of the first things I request is to see the organization chart. In general, missions and the business fundamentals plan will deploy according to the organization chart.

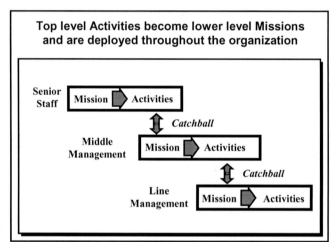

Before I continue the discussion of mission deployment, let me introduce you to a key Hoshin concept. In classic strategic planning, each level of the plan has a different title. For example; the vision is segmented into goals, goals are segmented into objectives, objectives are segmented into strategies, strategies are segmented into tactics, and tactics are segmented into tasks. This technique requires that each level of the plan have a different name. This can get very confusing especially since I have never found two planning consultants use the same set of terms. It also limits how deep the plan can be deployed because deploying it to another level requires creating a new name. Hoshin Kanri solves this problem by using term pairs. The term pairs are the same regardless of how deep the plan is deployed. For example, in Hoshin a mission is segmented into activities. When you deploy an activity down one level, it becomes that level's mission, which can be then further segmented into activities.

Hoshin also does not restrict you to specific term pairs[6]. Suppose you preferred the term "purpose" in place of "mission" and "key processes" in place of "activities." You would then use the term pair "purpose/key processes" on your business fundamentals plan. Each purpose can be segmented into lower level key processes. When you deploy a key process down one level, it becomes that level's purpose. Using term pairs allows the Hoshin plan to be deployed as deeply as you need to go.

The mission deployment process might best be illustrated by using an example. The fictional organization Rockford International employs 130 people. The top management staff consists of the President and managers for the functional areas of Operations, Marketing, Engineering, Finance, and Human Resources. Rockford International serves Southern California cabinetmakers by providing hinges and fasteners. Cabinetmakers have a critical need to respond to their customers quickly. They do not want to wait for parts to be delivered nor do they want to carry a huge inventory. Rockford International meets this need by providing their customers with next day delivery on all orders. With this situation in mind, the Rockford International management team used the mission format I described earlier to create the following mission:

> *To improve the responsiveness of Southern California cabinetmakers by providing hinges and fasteners with a one-day turnaround time.*

Rockford International's key customers are Southern California custom cabinetmakers, and their primary need is to be responsive to their customers. Rockford International meets this need by delivering parts within one day after they receive an order. When the management team felt comfortable with the mission, the President shared it with everyone during a monthly all-employee meeting. Each senior manager networked with people in their function to determine people's reaction to the mission.

The management team then met again to put the finishing touches on Rockford International's mission. The Marketing Manager reported that his people suggested that Rockford International's key customers were more focused than just "cabinetmakers." Because 70% of their business came from low volume, custom cabinetmakers, they wanted to insert the word "custom." The management team agreed. The Human Resources Manager indicated that his people thought the mission lacked "punch." Their suggestion was to delete the word "To" and begin the statement with the action verb "Improve". The team also agreed to this change. The Operations Manager wanted to make sure everyone understood that one day turnaround time was measured after receipt

---

[6] In the original Hoshin Kanri material I received back in 1986, the term pair objective/strategy was used for both business fundamentals and breakthrough plans. During one of my Hoshin planning training sessions for supervisors and managers, a production line supervisor pointed out that using the objective/strategy term pair for business fundamentals was confusing. He suggested that the term pair mission/activity be used instead. After discussing his proposal with the senior management team, we agreed and adopted the term pair mission/activity for business fundamentals and retained the term pair objective/strategy for breakthrough plans. I continue to use these term pairs today.

of the order. She suggested including the words "after receipt of order." The resulting discussion convinced her that the additional words tended to clutter the statement and that most people understood what "one day turnaround time" meant. Collectively, the management team agreed on this mission:

Improve the responsiveness of Southern California custom cabinetmakers by providing hinges and fasteners with one day turnaround time.

Now the management team had to determine how they were going to accomplish this mission. The President asked each senior manager to describe how their department would support the mission. The Operations Manager responded, "You can count on us to build products to orders and to ship on time." The Marketing Manager responded, "You can count on us to book orders and manage customer relationships." The Engineering Manager responded, "You can count on us to make sure products meet customer requirements and are reliable." The Finance Manager said, "You can count on us for the information necessary to make financial decisions." The Human Resource Manager said, "You can count on us to make sure we employ only good people and to train them so they will be successful." The President responded, "Great. I'm confident if everyone took care of their responsibilities, our mission will be achieved." He then instructed each senior manager to meet with their staff and obtain consensus on their functional missions.

One week later, the management team met again and shared their missions:

Operations: Maintain Rockford International customer satisfaction by consistently shipping quality products within one day of receiving an order.

Marketing: Manage Rockford International's revenue stream by supporting current customers and attracting new customers.

Engineering: Fuel Rockford International's growth by developing new products and assure customer satisfaction by providing technical support for current products.

Finance: Assure Rockford International's profitability by providing information so that sound business decisions can be made.

Human Resources: Assure Rockford International productivity by attracting, retaining, and training exceptional people and assure employee satisfaction by providing a safe, comfortable, equitable, and professional working environment.

Every manager listened intently as each shared their function's mission statement. The Operations Manager lobbied to have the Engineering Manager reverse the order of Engineering activities. The discussion was thought provoking, but they decided to let it stand for now. The President cautioned, "I just don't want us to get so focused on technical wizardry that we forget our bread and butter customers." The Finance Manager commented that Human Resources' mission was a mouthful. No changes were made,

however. The managers tested to see if there were any overlaps or gaps in assignments and then approved the statements. The Operations Manager stated, "Well, I think we now all know what is expected from each of us and our functions."

This example shows the give and take of mission development. In Hoshin, the back and forth discussion until consensus is reached is called "catchball." The next phase in the process would be for the function managers to take their missions and deploy them within their functions. Each mission would be segmented into key activities that would become the missions of lower level departments within the function. The process continues until every operational unit within the organization has a mission. Each mission will have direct linkage all the way back to the organization's mission.

The lower you deploy missions, the more likely the customer of the mission will reside within the organization. In fact, if you review the functional missions of Rockford International you will notice that most of them did not address custom cabinetmakers. The primary customer of the functional mission was the organization itself. At the lowest level, missions will be driven almost entirely by internal customers. Many of those customers will not be in the same functional area. As a result, the process of rationalizing department missions should include playing catchball side to side as well as up and down. The good news is that most of the people you need to talk to will be within walking distance.

The activities identified at the lowest level of mission deployment can also be thought of as the organization's key processes. These key processes must be managed and controlled to assure today's organizational success. They should always be constantly improved and are candidates for breakthrough improvements.

Based on my experience, I often do not document core processes on the lowest level planning tables. In other words, when deployment reaches a department with a supervisor and only individual contributors reporting to the supervisor or a self-managed team, I typically stop deployment and just document the department's mission. We haven't discussed performance measures yet, but in most cases front line department's business fundamentals can be managed by just using performance measures. For departments with multiple core processes and lots of people, however, it probably makes sense to also document the core processes. The key point is to keep it simple, but document core processes if it makes sense.

Business Fundamentals Planning Table

Up to this point, the discussion of missions is not much different from any other classical strategic planning process. They all expect you to create a mission and make sure everyone understands it. Effective planning techniques, however, take the process a little further. Clear ownership and performance measures need to be defined. So how does Hoshin address this issue? Remember that Hoshin is a set of forms and rules that facilitate the planning process. So let me introduce you to your first Hoshin form, the Business Fundamentals Planning Table.

In Chapter 7, Hoshin Tools, you will find two types of Business Fundamentals Planning Tables. On page 99 is a basic Business Fundamentals Planning Table, and on page 101 is another type of Business Fundamentals Planning Table. Now let's see how filling out these forms can facilitate the plan deployment process. Refer to the Business Fundamentals Planning Table on page 99 and assume we are documenting Rockford International's business fundamentals. The block titled Mission is self explanatory. Enter Rockford International's mission in this block. The owner of the mission has to be the President so enter the President's name enclosed in parentheses in the Mission block. The Situation block is helpful to justify and rationalize the mission. Enter information in the Situation block that will help people understand why it's important to accomplish the mission.

Each manager reporting to the President will be responsible for activities necessary to accomplish Rockford International's mission. Enter each activity, written in mission statement format, in the Activities section of the form. Identify each owner by enclosing their name in parentheses. To deploy the mission and activities, copy each Activity to the Mission field of a blank Business Fundamentals Planning Table. Now define the activities necessary to accomplish this mission. Notice how the linkage is obtained. Activities

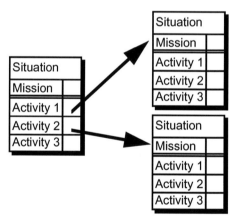

necessary to accomplish a higher order mission become the missions of the lower levels and can be further segmented into activities.

Deployment continues until you reach the lowest organizational units. At that point you might consider changing to the form shown on page 101. This form excludes the Situation statement. By the time you get to the lowest level, the Situation statement may have lost much of its value. This Business Fundamentals Planning Table adds columns for review cycles and data sources, and it allows more latitude in assigning ownership. A best practice is to make sure everyone in the department is listed somewhere on the

Business Fundamentals Planning Table. Of course you can use either form at any level. Use the form that works best for you[7].

If you decide to use the Business Fundamentals Planning Table shown on page 101, be careful to not over document the table. Each organizational unit probably employs tens to hundreds of processes to achieve its mission. You don't need to document all of them on the Business Fundamentals Planning Table. Keep the Pareto principle in mind. Most likely, three to five core processes are sufficient to document 80% of the total effort. Let the rest run on "automatic." Don't spend management time on them unless customer dissatisfaction occurs. Focus on the critical few not the less important many!

To see how the forms can be used to document the Hoshin business fundamentals plan, refer to the example plan for Rockford International on pages 105 through 108. The top level Business Fundamentals Planning Table (BFPT) is shown on page 106. This table is the documented result of the earlier discussion of how missions are deployed. Notice that Ira Cool owns the organization mission. This mission is segmented into the same number of activities as there are managers reporting to Ira. Each manager owns one activity. Notice how the situation statement includes information that justifies Rockford International's mission. After reading an effective Situation statement, a person should be able to say, "That makes sense. I understand why the mission is important."

Each activity on the top table is then deployed to another form where the activity on the top table becomes the mission of the lower table. In this case, the top BFPT would be deployed to five lower level BFPTs. Page 107 shows one of the five tables. It deploys the activity owned by Chris Builder, the operations manager. Notice that the mission on page 107 is verbatim with the activity owned by Chris on the top BFPT (page 106). If you use a manual Hoshin process, the verbatim rule is very important. If you don't enforce the rule, you will find that missions tend to change as they are deployed.

Referring to the organization chart on page 105, you will see that Chris Builder has three department supervisors reporting to her. As a result, Chris's BFPT has three activities, each one owned by one of her supervisors. Notice how the BFPT's situation statement is focused on the operations function.

Pat Shepard reports to Chris and manages the Materials department. Pat's BFPT is deployed from Chris's BFPT and shown on page 108. Notice that the second type[8] of BFPT form is used because this table is the last table in the deployment branch. This form does not have a situation statement and the activities listed are the core processes used to assure material is available to meet the production schedule. Notice that this

---

[7] The Hoshin software is based on the form on page 99. The form on page 101 is not used.

[8] As I mentioned before, I have stopped using the second type of BFPT (page 101) in my own Hoshin plans. I only use the first type (page 99). The prime reason is to keep it simple and avoid confusion. The second type of BFPT is still included in the handbook because it was part of the original Hoshin Kanri documentation and it's still useful if you implement a manual form of Hoshin without using software.

Total Quality Engineering

form allows for individual contributors to take responsibility for tracking performance measures.

Performing catchball during mission deployment is essential. The current organization management structure is the starting point for mission deployment, but it's not unusual for the deployment process to expose problems in that structure. For example, during catchball someone in another area might respond to the presentation of your mission with, "Hey, that's what I'm supposed to do." A statement like that indicates there is an overlap of responsibilities that should be resolved. Another typical response during catchball is a question like, "Who is responsible for collecting the data?" This question indicates there is a gap in the plan that should be filled. Catchball will also expose areas of focus that should be increased or reduced in priority. For example, you may find that a lower priority activity is fully staffed while a key core activity is complaining of being short staffed. Assuming that the people have similar skills, you may want to shift resources from the lower priority activity to the higher priority activity.

Catchball takes time because you are forced to build consensus, but it is well worth the effort. From a management point of view, it provides confidence that people are focused on the right things and assures that everyone understands how they contribute to the whole organization. People can trace their activities all the way up to the organization's mission.

You have probably noticed that there are sections on both Business Fundamentals Planning Tables that I have not mentioned. It's absolutely essential for everyone to understand their areas of responsibility. It's also essential for them to understand how well they are fulfilling that responsibility. Performance measures and/or deliverables are used to quantify performance and status. The Business Fundamentals Planning Table is completed by adding performance measures and/or deliverables, and they will be discussed in the next chapter.

Planning Table Numbering Systems

At this point, I would like to take a little aside and discuss how planning tables in a Hoshin plan are numbered. There are many ways to number the tables, but the key characteristics are that each table has a unique number and that the number contains information regarding the table's level in the plan. In what I will call "Classic" numbering, the top planning table is numbered "0" or is not numbered at all. The strategies or activities linked to the top table are numbered "1" through "n," where "n" is the number of strategies/activities.

In Classic numbering, the level of the plan is denoted by adding a "." to the number and then adding the number of the lower level strategy/Activity. For example, if Activity 2 on the top business fundamentals table is deployed to its own table and is segmented into four lower level activities, then the activities would be numbered 2.1, 2.2, 2.3, and 2.4. If table 2.3 is then further segmented into three lower level activities they would be numbered 2.3.1, 2.3.2, and 2.3.3.

Since deployment of business fundamentals often follows the organization chart, another numbering option is to just use the department number as the table's number. This can be useful in a manual process.

I will not spend much time on other numbering systems, because experience has shown that Classic numbering is preferred by most Hoshin users. TQE's original Hoshin software provided the option to use Classic or another system called Standard. Feedback from the software's users indicated that Standard numbering was practically never used. As a result the current version of the software only offers Classic numbering, and Classic numbering will be the format used throughout this handbook.

Notes

Chapter 4

Measuring Performance

How do I know I am doing a good job?

Two Types of Measures

You are driving your family across the state to visit your parents. You look down at the dashboard and verify that you have plenty of gas, the temperature gauge is in the green range, there are no warning lights, and the engine is purring. You have confidence your car is working fine. You just crossed over the river which means you are about halfway there. You are on schedule and you have confidence that you will arrive in time to enjoy another one of your Mother's great fried chicken dinners.

Suddenly, the oil warning light begins to flash on the dashboard. Luckily, you are near a service station so you pull over and ask if a mechanic is available. You're told the mechanic is on lunch break and should be back in a half-hour. With no other options, you wait. Finally the mechanic arrives and begins to troubleshoot your car. He informs you that it's not a big problem. You were just low on oil. You're soon on your way.

Unfortunately, the delay has really impacted your schedule. You are not even close to the little white church that marks the three-quarters point of your trip. You can visualize your parents sitting down to dinner without you and your family. Frustrated, you press down on the accelerator and the speedometer responds showing your increased speed. Maybe you can still arrive in time for dinner. Suddenly, you notice flashing red lights in your mirror. As you pull over, you are now convinced that you will be eating cold chicken.

This little story includes examples of the two types of measures we use all the time. The first type of measure is an indicator that provides real time information about the status of something. The car temperature, oil pressure, and speedometer are examples of this type.

Plotting the real time data over time creates a graph. In Hoshin Kanri this type of measure is called a performance measure. A key characteristic of a performance measure is that data can be plotted. Performance measure data tends to fall in a predictable range. Data falling outside that range probably indicates that something has changed. In Hoshin Kanri, the normal range is defined by action limits. An action limit is to process performance as the oil warning light is to the car's oil pressure.

The second type of measure indicates progress. In the story, crossing the river and passing the little white church were indicators of how far you had traveled. They can be thought of as milestones. In Hoshin Kanri, this type of measure is called a deliverable. A deliverable is the tangible result of completing a task.

Both performance measures and deliverables can have a goal. For a performance measure, a goal is the desired future value of the measure. For a deliverable, a goal is the deliverable's expected date of completion. While performance measures and deliverables can be used to track performance of both business fundamentals and breakthrough plans, performance measures are most often used in business fundamentals and deliverables are most often used in breakthrough plans. Each type of measure will now be described in more detail.

Performance Measures

There is an old adage that goes, "If you don't measure it, you can't manage it." There is another adage that goes, "Tell me how I'm going to be measured and I'll tell you how I'll perform." Measuring performance is one of the most difficult aspects of developing the Hoshin plan. Selecting the right measures can significantly improve organizational performance, but selecting the wrong measures can stifle effectiveness and create an environment of distrust.

I wish I had the ability to select only the right measures, but history tells me that I am at best mediocre at that skill. On the positive side, I'm pretty good at spotting the wrong measures so I can get rid of them quickly and select a new measure. Over time, I eventually build a set of measures that provide insight into performance and allow me to more effectively manage the organization. The trick is to observe human behavior that is triggered by performance measure selection. If the measure reinforces the behaviors you want, then it's good. If the measure reinforces behaviors you don't want, then get rid of it quickly.

People use many names to describe performance measures; Process Indicators and Metrics are just two examples. I will use the term performance measures, but feel free to use your own name for the measures.

To get started with the discussion of performance measures, think back to the previous chapter where we deployed the mission down to the lowest organizational units. At that point, deployment stopped and we documented the department's core processes. The question is, "What is a process?"

Joseph Juran[9] defines a process as any combination of machines, tools, methods, materials, and people employed to attain the qualities desired for products and services. Another simple definition of a process is *anything that causes something to change.* Using that definition, I think it's easy to see how everything we do can be thought of as a process. The process of accounting changes data into information. The process of marketing changes customer needs into orders. The process of management changes chaos into synergy (hopefully). Show me something that has changed and I will show you a process that made it happen. This means that the organization's mission and the mission of every organizational unit within the organization are also processes.

Performance of all processes can be measured and that includes biological processes like human life. Consider the situation of taking your baby daughter to the doctor for her periodic checkup. The nurse first takes her temperature and then measures her height and weight. The measured values are recorded and compared to what is normal for your daughter and other children her age. If all of the measurements fall into the normal range, then the doctor has confidence that your daughter is healthy. On the other hand, if your daughter has a temperature of 105 °F, it will trigger immediate action to understand the cause of the fever and bring her temperature back to normal.

I use the baby example, because a baby can't tell you that something is wrong. The only way to gain insight into her health is to measure vital signs and observe her behavior. Organizational processes also can't tell you how they are performing. You must measure performance in order to determine if the process is operating normally.

Generic measures for any process are *quality*, *cost*, and *delivery*. This is because all processes have customers, and quality, cost, and delivery are the critical elements of customer satisfaction. In other words, if the output costs too much, customers will not purchase it in the first place. If customers can't receive timely delivery, the order will be canceled. In addition, if the quality is such that customers perceive their expectations were not satisfied, the output will be returned and/or future purchases will go to another provider.

Because customer satisfaction is critical to organization success, the best measures are those provided by the customer. All customer perceptions are real and therefore customer based measures cannot be debated. There is a problem, however, of relying only on customer based measures. By the time you receive the first customer complaint, you probably have already delivered problems to many other customers. A good

---

[9] Source: "Quality Control Handbook, Third Edition" by Joseph M. Juran.

 Total Quality Engineering

technique is to select customer based measures at the highest levels of the plan and select internal measures that act as leading indicators of customer based measures for lower levels of the plan. Some examples are shown below:

Customer Based Measures	Internal Measures
Quality: % product warranty returns # product support calls	Quality: MTBF of ongoing reliability tests Usability index
Delivery: % cancellations due to late delivery % lost sales due to unavailability	Delivery: Average shipment time Days supply on hand
Cost: % lost sales due to high cost % complaints over operating cost	Cost: Material/Labor costs Supplies mark-up

All processes need at least one performance measure. However, to prevent optimizing one measure at the expense of the overall process health, most processes need a balanced set of measures[10] in the categories of quality, cost, and delivery. The test to determine if more than one measure is required is to answer the question, "Is there anything I can do to optimize this measure, but I know intuitively that it's the wrong thing to do?" If the answer to that question is "Yes," then a counter balancing measure is required. For example, suppose you work on a production line. Your mission is to build and ship products for paying customers. Your primary performance measure might be "# of units shipped." If the only way for you to meet your delivery requirement was to ship products that do not work, then you need a counter balancing measure. An example of a counter balancing measure for this situation might be, "% end of line rejects." Having both measures with equal priority assures that one measure will not be optimized at the expense of the other.

Selecting measures in the areas of quality, cost, and delivery will adequately measure most processes, but there is another area that should not be overlooked. The other key area is the impact on the people managing the process. Processes that are operating normally in the areas of quality, cost, and delivery might be doing so at the expense of employee morale or safety. For example, costs could be controlled by not hiring additional people, but the employed people may feel overworked and under supported. The low employee morale will ultimately show up in poor performance of measures in one or more of the other three measurement areas, but it's generally better to include a people measure. This will assure a balance between task management and people management. Typical people measures are morale survey results, employee comments on performance evaluations, and voluntary terminations or transfers.

---

[10] The concept of a balanced set of measures is the basis for the planning process called the Balanced Scorecard. How the Balanced Scorecard fits with Hoshin is discussed in Appendix A.

Characteristics of Effective Measures

So, how do you know you have a good performance measure? A good measure has three characteristics: 1) you can graph it, 2) it provides insight into process performance, and 3) it drives desired behavior.

If you can't create a graph of the measure, then it's not a good performance measure. Consider the measure of Customer Satisfaction. Every organization's management team that I have ever worked with all said they measured customer satisfaction. When I challenge them by asking what the level of customer satisfaction was last month the answer is often, "Pretty good." How do you plot "pretty good?" To have an effective measure you must count something, measure something, or create a ratio. You must end up with a number! A number can be plotted on a graph.

An effective measure must also provide insight into process performance. That means there is a causal relationship between the measured level and process inputs. For example, if you added a second shift to a production line you would expect to see the delivery measure go up. You would also see the cost measure go up and you would monitor the quality measure to assure the change did not negatively impact customer satisfaction. If you change process inputs and can't detect a change in the performance measure, then the measure may not have enough sensitivity to be effective.

When I was employed at HP, I found a classic example of a performance measure without proper sensitivity. I was auditing the Hoshin process of a production line and the line supervisor shared that one of his key measures was "Final Inspection Rejects." He proudly showed me a graph that had zero rejects for the past nine months. I too was impressed, but I asked him what would happen if he ever had a reject? His response was, "That won't happen." This told me that he was not using the measure to manage his process. After some additional questioning, I discovered that what he actually measured was "Rework Cost." The rework assured that there would be no rejects at final inspection. The graph of rework showed variation consistent with the varying quality of the line processes. The point is that a graph without variation can't be used to manage effectively. It doesn't have enough sensitivity. Will I show the Final Inspection Rejects graph to customers? You bet, but I will not use it to manage the production process.

The final characteristic of an effective measure is that it reinforces the human behavior you want. The mere fact that you measure something will change behavior. What management measures determines what's important. If you talk about quality but only measure monthly shipments then people will quickly learn that shipments are important and quality is optional. They will end up sacrificing quality to achieve delivery. If that's the behavior you want, then fine. If you don't want that behavior, then you need a counter balancing measure or a different measure.

Performance Measure Variation

Once you begin to collect data, it becomes obvious that data varies. Because data varies, it's impossible to predict the exact value of the next data element. Over time, however, you will observe that data tend to group around a central point. The science of statistics is based upon the propensity of data to group about a specific value. Translated into everyday language:

- Data varies.
- Individual data elements are unpredictable.
- Groups of data elements form a consistent pattern, and the probability of data elements falling within that pattern is predictable.

Here is an example to illustrate the concept:

- People live to different ages.
- No one knows how long they themselves will live.
- Insurance companies can tell with great accuracy what percentage of people will live to be 60, 65, 70, etc.

Fluctuations in data are caused by a large number of minute variations or changes: changes in materials, equipment, time, methods, environment, and the physical and mental state of process operators are just a few examples. Collectively, these small changes cause data to fluctuate in what is known as a "natural" or "normal" pattern. The mathematical model that describes this variation is known as the Normal Probability Distribution, Normal curve or Bell curve. I am not going to spend

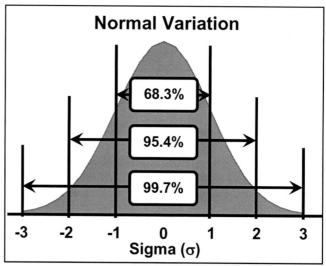

much time describing the characteristics of the Normal distribution. You can refer to any statistics book to understand this curve in more detail; but I believe every manager should understand its concepts. The Normal distribution is characterized by its Mean (average) and Standard Deviation (sigma). The Mean is a measure of central tendency and the Standard Deviation is a measure of data spread.

The unique aspect of the Normal distribution is that essentially all (99.7%) of the data points fall within ±3 Standard Deviations from the Mean. This infers that any data point falling outside that range is most likely a data point not consistent with natural process variation. As long as data falls within the ±3 Standard Deviation range, we are confident the process is operating normally. Statisticians use the term "in statistical control" to describe data variation that is consistent with the Normal distribution.

Goals and Action Limits

To effectively implement Hoshin Kanri you must understand the difference between goals and action limits. Incorrectly using them is one of the biggest mistakes new Hoshin users make (Chapter 7). The distinctions between goals and action limits are rooted in the concept of Process Capability[11]. Action limits are computed based on process capability while goals are selected based on factors independent of process capability.

Recognize that every process is ideally designed to deliver the results it's delivering. Those results may or may not be what you desire. If the results do not meet your expectations, there is no amount of threats or encouragement that will make the output change. The process is what it is. If you don't like the current results, then you must change the process.

Performance measures are used within Hoshin to track performance of activities (processes). The natural variation of performance measures defines what's normal or what can be reasonably expected from the current process design. Hoshin defines action limits as the ±3 Standard Deviation limits of the performance measure's natural variation. As long as data variation remains within the action limits, we have reasonable confidence that the process is operating normally.[12] That means that the process is operating as it was designed.

If process variation shows a data point outside the action limits, then the most logical explanation is that the process has changed. Action should be taken to understand the root cause of the abnormal variation. If the change is in the "bad" direction, then Action should be initiated to bring process performance back to normal. If the change is in the "good" direction, then Action should be taken to capture the unexpected gain and standardize the new process.

The main point to remember is that as long as a process is operating normally, management does not need to intervene. The process is considered to be "running on auto-pilot."

---

[11] Process Capability (Cpk) is a measure of how well a process meets its designed requirements. Refer to the Memory Jogger II (listed in the bibliography) or other texts on Quality Control for more information.

[12] One data point falling outside the 3 SD limits is only one of many statistical tests for normality. You should research and understand the other tests for normality. For a quick overview, refer to the Memory Jogger II (listed in the bibliography) or a statistics text for more in-depth understanding.

Action limits are based on a measure's historical performance. That means you must have data before action limits can be computed. Most statisticians suggest that you need 20-30 data points before you can compute action limits. My minimum number is twelve data points. That's because most organization performance measures are collected on a monthly basis and I don't like to go more than one year without computing action limits.

If you don't have historical data, then I suggest you not use action limits or set them to a value that is not easily exceeded. You should trigger action only when you have confidence the process had changed. You don't want people trying to explain normal variation.

The fact that a process is operating normally and performance measures are within the computed action limits does not mean the process is performing at desired levels. The desired future level of performance is called the goal.

While action limits are computed based on process capability, goals are selected based on desired future levels of performance. Goals are not restricted to current process capability or limitations. Goals are based on competitive pressure, customer requirements, or desired organization growth. Selecting a goal, however, does not automatically change performance. To achieve goal levels of performance, processes will have to be systematically improved over time.

This figure shows the relationship between action limits and goals. In most cases, action limits are related to business fundamentals while goals are related to breakthrough plans. If current performance meets goal requirements, the performance is held by the action limits. If current performance does not meet goal requirements, then the goal

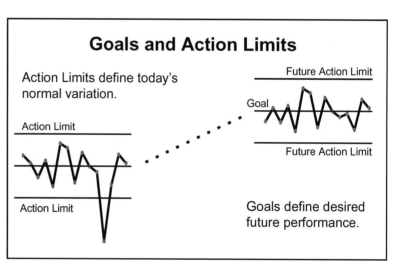

provides the performance gap necessary to drive process improvement. The improvement effort is typically documented in the breakthrough plan. Once process performance is capable of meeting goal levels, the gain is standardized into business fundamentals and new action limits are computed.

At this point, I need to address the issue of constant process improvement. All processes should be constantly improved. Process owners should have an intimate understanding of their processes. They should always be searching for ways to improve. These

activities, however, need not be documented in the Hoshin plan. The essence of business fundamentals is maintaining performance. The essence of breakthrough planning is significant improvement. I will address the case of department specific breakthrough planning in the next chapter. Unless a department's mission statement specifically documents the activities of ongoing improvement teams, my suggestion is to leave continuous improvement activity out of the Hoshin plan. Include continuous improvement in your values and expect continuous improvements to occur, but keep the Hoshin plan focused on the critical few things necessary for organization success.

Deliverables

A deliverable is the tangible result of completing a job or task. For example, the deliverable of the task to paint your fence is a "painted fence." Until the fence is completely painted, the task is not complete. A deliverable is an attribute measure – it either is or is not complete.

Deliverables often depend on the completion of other deliverables. For example, fence painting can't start until you have purchased the paint, and it's a good idea to measure the fence and estimate how much paint is needed before purchasing the paint. A set of related deliverables can be described as a project. Since the project typically has a desired date of completion, each deliverable within the project will have a completion date goal. Plotting the expected start date and completion date for each deliverable of the project creates a Gantt chart[13].

The wording used to describe a deliverable can be important. For best results, the deliverable should be described as the result of the task instead of the task itself. Consider the examples below:

Paint fence.	vs.	Fence painted.
Investigate supplier alternatives.	vs.	Supplier selected.
Travel to New York.	vs.	Arrive in New York.
Conduct meeting to sign contract.	vs.	Contract signed.

The deliverable descriptions on the left describe the task while the descriptions on the right describe what you have when the task is complete. It's much easier to test the descriptions on the right for completeness. When probing for status of the descriptions on the left, you will typically receive progress reports that describe ongoing activity. This can make it difficult to determine actual status.

---

[13] For more information on Gantt charts, refer to the Memory Jogger II in the bibliography or any project management text.

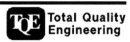

The Hoshin review process will be discussed in more detail in Chapter 6, but a best practice is to never have a deliverable span multiple review periods. In other words, avoid creating a deliverable where status is described as "percent complete." If a task spans multiple review periods, then break it into smaller tasks with deliverables that are scheduled for completion in each review period. Percent complete evaluation tends to hide problems, but a single late deliverable will quickly identify the need for corrective action.

In most cases, deliverables will be associated with Hoshin breakthrough plans, but they can be used for business fundamentals. In breakthrough plans, deliverables are used to provide status of improvement projects. In business fundamentals, deliverables are used to track periodic events that don't lend themselves well to a graph. For example, if my business fundamental is to conduct a training class once each month, deliverables could be created for each class. As long as each class is completed on schedule, I have confidence that my process to conduct training classes is operating normally.

Completing the Business Fundamentals Plan

In Chapter 3 we began the process of developing the Hoshin business fundamentals plan by defining the organization mission and deploying it to each organizational unit within the organization. Each mission/activity had a Situation statement that described why the mission/activity was important and an owner was selected that will be accountable to assure the mission/activity is achieved. To complete the Hoshin business fundamentals plan, each mission/activity needs performance measures that will provide insight into how well the mission/activity is being achieved. A general rule is that each mission/activity should have at least two and often four or more counter-balanced measures.

Review the example business fundamentals plan for Rockford International and Great Northern in Chapter 8. Notice how each table describes the expectations of a specific organizational unit and could stand alone. Notice how the business fundamentals plan deploys the organization mission all the way down to the lowest levels. Notice that each owner can show how their activities contribute to the organization's success. Notice that clear measures of success exist at each level. Business Fundamentals Planning Tables act as management's control panel for organization performance. They define what activities are important and how you know if those activities are performing well.

Values

There is nothing in any of the Hoshin literature that I have studied that addresses the concept of "Values," but I have learned that establishing shared values is a powerful complement to Hoshin. I will not go into a lengthy discussion of the benefit of values. There are a number of good books on the subject, and I have listed some of them in the bibliography. Simply stated, a value is something that you will never compromise. Values are developed at the emotional level and help define right and wrong.

Stephen Covey[14] goes so far as to say that values (he actually calls them principles) are the keys to becoming highly effective. Most organizations have done a good job of establishing values. Don't throw away your values when you implement Hoshin. Use them to provide an operating conscience for Hoshin. Values support Hoshin by establishing the normal set of expected behaviors. Values empower employees to carry out activities described in the business fundamentals and annual plan without the need for management approval. As long as the values are not compromised, employees should be free to make decisions on their own. Only issues that might compromise one or more of the values need to be escalated to management's attention. To illustrate the point consider the value set below:

Customer satisfaction: 100% customer satisfaction is the goal of every employee.
Fiscal responsibility: We manage within our budget.

It's reasonable to expect people to fulfill their mission most of the time without compromising either of these two values. On the other hand, I'm sure you can also visualize situations where achieving true 100% customer satisfaction would cause you to exceed your financial budget. You may find a win-win situation where neither Value is compromised, but most likely one will take priority over the other. The Value that takes priority depends on the situation. In one case, your financial status may be such that you cannot afford any extra expense. As a result, you will have to suffer the negative impact of customer dissatisfaction. In another case, the customer may be so critical to future success that you are willing to take a loss in the short term. Decisions like these require management attention. Management does not necessarily have any better insight into the problem than you do, but they do have overall responsibility for business success, and this is the kind of decision where you need their support.

The organization and every organizational unit within the organization should have a set of values. Corporate values are good and provide direction for other value sets, but they do not necessarily translate directly into the Personnel, Maintenance, or Accounting departments. Each department should have its own set of values based on organizational responsibilities and the people leading and working in the department. A process to create department values is found in Appendix F.

---

[14] Source: "The 7 Habits of Highly Effective People" by Stephen R. Covey.

The Main Benefit of Business Fundamentals and Values

Every model of TQM describes the concept of employee empowerment. Push decision making to the lowest levels. Those closest to the problem know best how to solve it. Trust employees to make the right decisions. It all sounds so good and simple, but most senior executives wince at the thought of allowing front line employees to make decisions that could cripple the organization financially. The TQM zealots accuse them of not trusting employees and wanting to keep all power for themselves.

My observation is that most senior managers want employees to take more ownership, but the risk of employees making a huge mistake far outweighs the empowerment benefits. It's not a lack of trust; it's a lack of confidence that employees have the data and experience to make sound decisions that include the best interest of the organization.

Now imagine a situation where every manager, supervisor, and self-managed team has a Business Fundamentals Planning Table documenting their group's responsibilities. The tables have been catchballed up, down, and across the organization. Clear consensus has been reached on what is expected, and how performance is measured and controlled. Action limits have been set consistent with the group's competence and past performance. Each Business Fundamentals Planning Table will then define an envelope of responsibilities that management feels confident employees can handle by themselves. Business Fundamentals Planning Tables allow managers to back away from detail and micro-management. As long as employees are meeting their responsibilities, maintaining performance measures within the action limits, and not compromising organization values, then management involvement can be reduced to periodic review of status. Employees are truly empowered within the boundaries of the Business Fundamentals Planning Table.

The primary benefit of well-established business fundamentals and values is that they free managers from daily details and allow them to take a more strategic view of where the organization needs to go. Managers can now manage *on* the business instead of managing *in* the business. This leads us to the next phase of Hoshin: breakthrough planning.

Chapter 5

Vision and Breakthrough Plans

Where are we going and how are we going to get there?

What are Strategic Decisions?

Managers make hundreds of decisions each day. The majority of decisions are in response to a problem. Decisions result in an answer. For example, managers will decide to hire or not hire people, buy or lease equipment, ship or hold customer products, or select the paint color for the lunch room. Although these decisions are necessary and may require immediate attention, in the long run they have only a small impact on the organization's success. The problem is that even if you were 100% correct on every one of these tactical decisions, the organization could still be lost to an unexpected market shift. At the turn of the 20th century, the best buggy whip manufacturer in the world was experiencing a loss of sales just like all the other buggy whip manufacturers. Customers were shifting from horse drawn carriages to automobiles and as a result the market for buggy whips was evaporating. Outside circumstances can overwhelm an organization in spite of how well it manages its daily operations.

Tactical decisions belong in business fundamentals. With strategic decisions, we're not looking for the right answer; we're looking for the right question. In tactical decisions, the situation is clear and the decision criteria are understood. What remains is selecting the most economical solution. With strategic decisions, the situation is not clear; it must be researched and understood. Once the situation is understood, the organization must create a plan to react to predicted situation changes or change the situation to better fit the organization's desires. Once the plan's direction is established, the organization must align everyone's effort in order to achieve organization goals. I think Peter Drucker describes the distinction between tactical and strategic decisions as well as anyone:

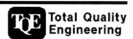

The important decisions, the decisions that really matter, are strategic. They involve either finding out what the situation is, or changing it, either finding out what the resources are or what they should be. These are the specifically managerial decisions. Anyone who is a manager has to make such strategic decisions, and the higher his level in the management hierarchy, the more of them he must make.

Strategic decisions--whatever their magnitude, complexity or importance--should never be taken through problem-solving. Indeed, in these specifically managerial decisions, the important and difficult job is never to find the right answer, it's to find the right question. For there are few things as useless--if not as dangerous--as the right answer to the wrong question.

Nor is it enough to find the right answer. More important and more difficult is to make effective the course of action decided upon. Management is not concerned with knowledge for its own sake; it's concerned with performance. Nothing is as useless therefore as the right solution that is quietly sabotaged by the people who have to make it effective. And one of the most crucial jobs in the entire decision making process is to assure that decisions reached in various parts of the business and on various levels of management are compatible with each other, and consonant with the goals of the whole business.[15]

The last paragraph in Drucker's quote is very important. Most organizations do a good job of determining their strategic direction. The issue is not deciding what to do but doing it! I have seen great strategic plans that simply sat on the shelf until it was time to create next year's strategic plan. In my opinion, the effort to create the plan was wasted. Hoshin helps prevent this problem and acts to achieve *excellence in execution*. Hoshin helps make the strategic plan an integral part of business management. In addition, the PDCA aspect of Hoshin helps fine tune the plan as more information is received. An organization with a mediocre plan that executes excellently will always beat an organization with a great plan that does not execute. Hoshin will not tell you what to do, but it will help you achieve what you decide to do.

This chapter describes breakthrough planning. Breakthrough plans document how the organization will change the way it currently does business to meet the needs of the future. Breakthrough plans are not continuous improvement. Breakthrough plans involve strategic initiatives and bold, stretch objectives. In most cases, it's not obvious how you will achieve breakthrough objectives. You will know the general direction, but many of the specific action steps will be developed as you go. Of course the better your data, the more likely you will start in the right direction.

---

[15] Source: "The Practice of Management" by Peter F. Drucker.

The Power of Vision

Breakthrough plans are based on the organization's vision of the future. In recent years, there has been a lot of material published on the power of vision. If an organization can identify a unifying theme that everyone buys into, it can be very powerful; but what is an effective vision? In the first place, a vision has to be visual. The whole purpose of a vision statement is to describe the future in visual terms. Effective visions make use of

Vision
➤ A compelling image of the future that draws people to it. 
➤ Makes use of metaphors, models, pictures, comparisons and analogies.
➤ Appeals to people's emotions.
➤ Provides a sense of purpose, direction, and a reason to carry on.

metaphors and imagery to paint a picture. They appeal to people's emotions and inspire a need for action.

Most strategic planning consultants step through the creation of mission, vision, and values almost in lock step. The result is a mission and vision that are difficult to tell apart. The statements are so generic that they could be used for any organization. Consider the below two statements:

The **Mission** of The Organization is to serve our customers with the highest levels of customer satisfaction, providing price competitive products developed and delivered on time by our innovative, talented, dedicated, and empowered workforce.

Vision: Our customers are fully satisfied with our products and services; they consider us a responsive supplier. Our workforce is empowered and always striving to do their best. Within our community, we are viewed as a good citizen. Our internal processes are always functional and striving for the highest quality possible. We use TQM to achieve continuous improvement in everything we do.

I can't count the number of mission and vision statements like the ones above I have seen. The first conclusion I draw when comparing the two statements is that the organization is obviously doing "bad" today. The mission serves customers by delivering "the highest levels of customer satisfaction" yet the vision has customers "fully satisfied." Does that mean today's "highest levels" do not yield "fully satisfied" customers? The mission uses an "empowered workforce" but the vision describes future employees as "empowered and always striving to do their best." Does that mean they are not empowered and strive to do their best today? Mission and vision statements like these don't motivate performance. They can actually demoralize employees; but more often than not they are just ignored. Employees view these statements as the result of an out of touch management team creating a feel-good document for themselves.

Unless people can internalize the mission and vision statements, they will not use them in daily decisions. If they do not use the statements to guide their decisions, then is not the

 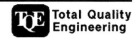

whole exercise just a waste of time? One of the best tests I have found to see if people have internalized their mission and vision statements is to ask them to quote it. The vast majority of people I challenge can't quote their organization's mission and vision. Most of the senior managers that were involved in creating the statements can't quote them either. I have already talked about techniques for creating a memorable mission in the previous chapter. Creating a memorable vision is a little more difficult but it can be ten times more powerful.

Martin Luther King Jr.'s famous "I have a dream" speech was filled with excellent vision examples. He spoke of a future "where little black boys and black girls will be able to join hands with little white boys and white girls and walk together as sisters and brothers." While selling the NASA space program to Congress, John F. Kennedy cited an objective of "before the decade is out, landing a man on the moon and returning him safely to the earth." Both of these statements provide a clear visual image of what was to be. The images are easily remembered. Of course the intent of King's speech was to achieve racial equality, and Kennedy wanted to regain technological superiority over Russia. The images of children walking hand in hand and astronauts returning from the moon appeal to peoples' emotions. You might forget the exact words that describe the objective to achieve racial equality, but you will not forget the image of the children. You might forget the exact words that describe the objective to obtain technical dominance over Russia, but the image of a space capsule splashing into the ocean after a successful lunar landing mission will be clear.

There is no secret recipe for creating visions, but there are some common themes. King's vision addressed correcting a morally wrong situation. Kennedy's vision can be described as *being the first*, it addressed a competitive situation. Other themes include *significant growth* and *creating something new*. Organization visions tend to fall into two categories. Market leaders tend to have "world changing" visions while market trailers tend to "target the leader."

In the early 1970s, Cannon was a new player in the copier business. Xerox was the market leader. Cannon had a very simple vision, *Beat Xerox!* They almost did. Xerox responded to the market pressure and defined a vision to be *the first US organization directly targeted by the Japanese to not only recover but to regain its market share.* Xerox went on to win one of the first Baldrige awards. In 1960, startup shoe manufacturer Nike wanted to *crush Adidias*. Nike is a powerhouse today.

In 1900, Ford was the biggest auto maker and had a vision to *democratize the automobile.* Ford wanted to see a Model-T in every garage. In 1950, Boeing was the dominate aircraft manufacturer and wanted to *bring the world into the jet age.* In 1980, Coca Cola's vision was to *put a Coke within arms reach of everyone in the world.* Independent of market leader or trailer status, I think you can see how each of these visions influenced the organization's decisions. Visions drive action.

Effective visions inspire action. They focus on a specific objective and appeal to everyone. A vision should address how everyone will be better off when it's achieved. Sounds good, but how do you create a vision? Some strong leaders already have their vision of the future and are very effective at getting others to buy-in and support it. If you are not fortunate enough to already be working for someone like that, you will need to spend some time with data before the vision will spontaneously appear. I'm not being facetious. Visions come from the creative side of our brains. I don't fully understand the process, but I've learned to "wallow in the data." After a while, themes begin to appear, and what must be done becomes obvious. The process starts with understanding the current situation and predicting a future situation.

Define the Situation

The vision process begins with an understanding of the current situation. There are hundreds of forces pulling the organization in multiple directions. Some forces are controllable and others are not. The ability of the organization to understand these forces and change processes to adapt or shape future forces is a critical success factor.

Numerous books have been written on how to establish winning business strategies, and I am not going to compete with authors like Peter Drucker, Michael Porter, Joseph Juran, Tom Peters and other experts. It seems that every issue of the *Harvard Business Review* contains one or more articles addressing some element of strategic planning. I encourage you to study the literature available on classical strategic planning, but all strategic planning begins with an analysis of the current situation and then

Strategic Planning Questions[16]

Today	In the Future
Which customers do you serve today?	Which customers will you serve in the future?
Through what channels do you reach customers today?	Through what channels will you reach customers in the future?
Who are your competitors today?	Who will be your competitors in the future?
What is the basis for your competitive advantage today?	What will be the basis for your competitive advantage in the future?
Where do your margins come from today?	Where will your margins come from in the future?
What skills or capabilities make you unique today?	What skills or capabilities will make you unique in the future?

attempts to predict what the future situation will be. Based on the predicted future situation, the organization defines the key things that must be changed or implemented in order to assure the organization remains viable in the future.

---

[16] Source: "Competing for the Future" by Gary Hamel & C.K. Prahalad, Harvard Business Review, July-August 1994.

Hoshin

TQE Total Quality Engineering

Hoshin is a methodology driven by data. The more you understand and can quantify your current situation, the better you will be able to predict what your future situation will be. It's important to collect real data and not let opinions and anecdotes define your breakthrough objectives.

Most strategic planning sessions are conducted off-site in an intense two or three day session. This technique is very effective in improving the teamwork of the management team, but they are separated from the information necessary for effective decisions. Opinions take the place of data during these meetings. The person with the best debating skill (sometimes the one with the loudest voice) tends to dominate and influence the direction of the group. Consensus is difficult because it's hard to separate opinions from their owners. For example, if you have high regard for an individual you will be more apt to believe their opinions are facts. On the other hand, if you do not trust someone their opinions will always be clouded with perceived hidden agendas.

A technique to inject data into plan development is to hold planning meetings on-site. Instead of one big meeting, consider many shorter meetings spread out over two to four weeks. When data are analyzed and presented, as many questions are raised as are answered. With frequent short meetings, questions can be answered with a different set of data and/or analysis at the next meeting.

Each organization has its own particular set of data required for strategic planning, but in general data should address the following key areas: 1) Sales and sales trends, 2) Customer satisfaction and trends, 3) Competitors and predicted moves, 4) Technology trends, 5) Supplier trends, and 6) Organization core competencies. Data from each of these areas should be segmented and analyzed until it's obvious to everyone what opportunities exist. The focus on data helps remove personalities from the decision making process. It also improves buy-in because decisions can be supported with data, not opinions. I will briefly touch on each of these key data areas.

You would think sales and sales trends would be obvious to every senior manager; but I have stopped being surprised by senior managers that could not name the organization's three biggest customers and what volume of sales those customers represent. There is always someone in the organization that does have an intimate knowledge of sales activity, and that person or department should be enlisted to support the sales analysis process. There are numerous ways to display the data. My personal preference is to create a matrix of sales dollars by customer or customer segment and product or service. Order the columns such that the biggest customer or customer segment is at the left of the matrix and order the rows such that the biggest product or service is at the top.

If your organization sells to a few customers, then use actual customer names in the matrix. If you sell to a broad customer base, then segment customers into similar categories appropriate for your business. For example, a movie theater might segment by the customer's age, and a product manufacturer might segment by geographic location.

There is no *right* segmentation. Try different segmentations until one shows a Pareto relationship and you feel it provides insight to understanding your customer base. Define the product or service in the same manner. If you have just a few products, then use the actual product or service names, otherwise group them into families.

Sales Dollar Matrices

Product	Market Segment			%
	B	A	C	
C	80	40	10	50%
B	40	15	12	26%
A	35	10	18	24%
%	60%	25%	15%	260

Current

Product	Market Segment			%
	A	B	C	
A				
B				
C				
%				

Future

An example of a sales dollar matrix is shown above. The first matrix defines the current status. The second matrix predicts the future status. You will not be able to complete the future matrix until later in the planning process so for now let's just focus on the current matrix. Notice that market segment B accounts for 60% of the total sales dollars and that Product C provides 50% of the organization's sales. This matrix should be based on real sales data. The information should be readily available to you. Avoid estimating the cell values. Spend the time to segment and quantify the data accurately. Unless you deliver all of your products and services directly, a matrix of products by distribution channel or customer segment by distribution channel could also be enlightening. Develop as many matrices as necessary to accurately quantify where today's sales are derived.

Recreate each sales matrix as if you were your top two or three competitors. This may be difficult. Your competitors probably will not share their sales data with you. Make sure you get a good mix of marketing and sales people involved so that you can make educated estimates of sales volume. Trying to create the competitor matrices usually exposes a weakness in the organization's competitive intelligence process. This weakness will likely trigger breakthrough efforts to develop or improve this capability or core competency.

If you can complete the sales matrices, you should have a good idea of how your sales compare to your key competitors' sales. The exercise will expose customer segments where you are strong and your competitors are weak and vice versa. It will also expose areas where you are battling for market share.

The next step in analyzing sales data is to identify the customer needs of each market segment. Use classical quality tools like Brainstorming and Affinity Diagrams to help identify the key customer needs. By all means, do include actual customer information collected from interviews, focus groups, and surveys. Most people find it helpful to create relationship matrices showing which customer needs are required by each customer segment. By completing the matrices, it will probably be apparent that different segments have different needs. One segment might have a strong need for "speed" while another segment could tolerate a lower "speed" if they could get the product or service at a lower cost.

User Needs Matrix

Need	Market Segment		
	A	B	C
Large	O	●	
Fast	●		●
Low Cost		O	●

O Want ● Must

Now that you have identified the key customer needs, create matrices that display how well you and your competitors are satisfying those needs today. To create the matrices for the future, you will need additional data and a little "imagineering."

Identify External Forces

The organization's future will be impacted by many things that are outside its control. Technology advances, changes in government regulations, new and existing competitors, societal issues, and the employee resource pool are just a few examples. These forces will impact each matrix created in the previous steps.

A good step to identify forces that might affect the organization is to conduct a brainstorming session with a diverse cross-section of organization managers and process experts. List the external forces and try to support each one with publicly available literature. This helps remove opinion based input. Once the list is completed, try to predict the impact each force will have on your future matrices. Assume the organization will operate in the future exactly the same as it operates today, that is business fundamentals will not change. This exercise exposes areas where the organization's future is threatened and areas of opportunity that the organization could exploit to its advantage. The premise, however, is that business fundamentals will most likely need to change in order to remain competitive in the future.

Identify Internal Forces and Core Competencies

All organizations have capabilities or competencies that allow them to deliver products and services that satisfy real customer needs. A core competency is typically defined as capability that sets the organization apart from its competition.

Identification of core competencies usually begins with another brainstorming session. Be sure to not let the session degrade into a "feel good" exercise. I have yet to facilitate one of these sessions where the group did not identify "our people" as a key core competency. When I probe for a better understanding, I learn that there is nothing unique about their people. They hire from the same labor pool as their competitors, their hiring process is nothing to brag about, and their training and mentoring processes are typical of other organizations. How can their people be a core competency? On the other hand, if the organization has specific processes that attract and retain only highly skilled people, then it may very well be a core competency. A core competency sets the organization apart from its competition.

Using the above definition of a core competency, it's not unusual to have a very small list. On the other hand, an organization could have twenty or more key processes essential to delivering products and services to its customers. List the core competencies and key processes in a matrix showing their relationship to satisfying customer needs today.

The next step is to identify the internal forces that work to enhance or degrade the core competencies and key processes. Examples include an aging workforce, education level of new hires, equipment reliability, and corporate initiatives and mandates. With this information, predict the impact your core competencies and key processes will have on future customer satisfaction. This will expose areas of strength and weakness.

Summarize SWOT and Crystallize the Vision

Now that you have all this data and predictions of the future, it's time to do something with it. Before *analysis paralysis* sets in, step back and summarize what you know. What **strengths** does the organization have that you want to protect and could be a base for future growth? What **weakness** is the organization saddled with that could prove to be devastating if not improved? What **opportunities** are present for the organization to enter new markets or capture significant gains in current markets? What **threats** exist that the organization must defend to maintain or grow its business?

Each organization will obviously have many items in each SWOT category, but one or two items in one category will usually be significant. I can't describe a systematic process to achieve creative understanding of SWOT and the subsequent creation of the organization's vision; but I have witnessed it happen many times. It does not always

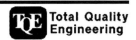

happen in one meeting. Sometimes it takes numerous meetings before consensus builds. It usually begins with someone saying, "You know, if we could only..." That comment is built upon by another comment and soon ideas are flowing freely. After a while, someone makes a statement that everyone feels captures the flavor of the discussion and a vision is born.

To illustrate the vision process, let me again use the Rockford International example. During a strategic planning meeting, the management team was reviewing data collected by their sub-committee teams. The teams included a marketing team, a supplier management team, a technology team, and a human resources team. The teams had done a great job of quantifying Rockford International's current business position and identifying what might happen if Rockford International did not change the way it did business.

The data and analysis showed that Rockford International enjoyed a very strong position within Southern California. Eighty percent of Southern California custom cabinetmakers recognized Rockford International's name and preferred to use Rockford International products whenever possible. Sixty-three percent of all custom work completed in the past year used Rockford International products. The analysis also showed that new construction in Southern California had been on the decline for the past two years and was expected to decline even more during the next three years. Construction in other areas of the US and in other countries was growing; but custom work was declining across the nation. Purchases of ready made cabinets from home supply retailers were on the rise. Rockford International's core competency of next day delivery served local custom cabinetmakers very well, but it would be of little value selling to large discount retailer chains. They needed products with significantly lower cost and higher reliability. Volume purchases would minimize the benefit of next day delivery.

As the management team studied the data, the Engineering Manager commented that one strategy would be to use Rockford International's core competency to win 100% of the custom cabinet market. The Marketing Manager countered by stating that a small slice of a big pie is probably better than all of a small pie. Other options were proposed but someone always had a counter point and they seemed to be going nowhere. The mood dropped until the President began describing his visits to job sites. He commented that he could walk into almost any Southern California construction site and see Rockford International products being used. He contrasted that to job sites he visited in Texas where he saw no Rockford International products. The Marketing Manager added that if we want to expand outside of Southern California, then Rockford International needs to quit selling direct to builders and leverage sales through retailers. The President responded that it would be nice to see Rockford International products being used throughout the US. The Finance Manager then asked why sales needed to stop at the US border. Why not sell products throughout the world? The discussion seemed to strike a resonate cord with the management team. The energy level in the room increased, and it was clear people were getting exited about expanding Rockford International's market.

Then the Human Resource Manager reminded everyone that the organization's name already included the word "International." He suggested they live up to their name and become an international organization. The comment appealed to everyone. A vision was born.

Translate the Vision into a Long Range Plan

So far, I have not described anything that is unique to the Hoshin process. There are many different ways for organizations to develop a vision. Most US organizations actually do a good job of creating a vision and determining what must be accomplished to achieve the vision. They fall down on execution.

Hoshin Kanri is not a process to "figure out what to do." Hoshin Kanri is a plan

Long Range Plan

➢ Covers five, ten even twenty years.
➢ Acts to quantify the vision.
➢ Limited deployment, but widely communicated.
➢ Changes little from year to year.

implementation process. Hoshin picks up where other planning processes stop. Hoshin helps organizations deploy and execute "what they want to do."

After the vision is defined, the next step is to translate it into something that can be acted upon. Most visions tend to be wordy. They are filled with emotional elements, and it's not always clear when the vision is achieved. To make the vision actionable, it should be crystallized into a concise objective statement. The objective should have clear measures of success defined and ownership assigned. In addition, the strategies necessary to achieve the objective should be identified. Owners and performance measures should also be assigned for each strategy.

The long range plan, sometimes referred to as the strategic plan, describes how the organization expects to transform itself into what it *should* be in the future. The long range plan should cover at least a three to five year window. Many progressive organizations have long range plans looking out ten or even twenty years. The vision must be communicated throughout the organization. It should be mentioned at almost every organization-wide meeting and periodically included in other organization communication vehicles. The vision points the direction; but the long range plan converts the vision into action.

Hoshin facilitates development and deployment of the long range plan with a form. The form is called a Hoshin Planning Table, and a blank form is shown on page 91. Notice that this form looks very much like the Business Fundamentals Planning Table found on page 99. The primary differences are the form's title and the replacement of the words

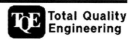

"Mission" with "Objective", "Activities" with "Strategies", and "Action Limits" with "Goals". Other than the label changes, a Hoshin Planning Table is used just like a Business Fundamentals Planning Table.

Performance Measures or Deliverables

In business fundamentals, almost every mission/activity can be tracked with a balanced set of performance measures. As long as performance remains within the action limits then you have confidence that processes are operating normally. Simply flashing the graphs is usually sufficient to determine if everything is OK.

In breakthrough plans (both Long Range and Annual) performance improvement is the result of successful implementation of a series of tasks or deliverables. Deliverables can be thought of as milestones along the implementation path. A deliverable is defined as a tangible result of a task. For example, the deliverable of the objective (or project) to prepare a meal is the act of consuming the meal. Until you actually sit down and start eating, the deliverable is not achieved.

Both performance measures and deliverables are used to track performance of breakthrough plans. The highest level tables tend to use mainly performance measures with clear goals. Measures should be selected that will show the result of improvement activities. In other words, you should be able to see before and after regions on the graph.

The lower you go in the plan, the more deliverables will be used. Since the lowest level tables in the annual plan will really document an improvement project, they are almost exclusively tracked using deliverables. Between the top and bottom planning tables, a mixture of performance measures and deliverables will be used. This concept will be discussed in more detail later.

Develop the Long Range Plan

To illustrate how the Hoshin Planning Table is used to document the long range plan, let's again use the Rockford International example. Refer to Rockford International's long range plan found on page 109. Notice the title of the form has changed. This form is titled "Long Range Plan". The situation field includes the essential information collected during vision development to justify why the long range plan is important. Notice how the situation field documents key elements of Rockford International's SWOT analysis.

The Objective field contains a concise statement that captures the essence of the vision. In the Rockford International example, the objective is to expand Rockford International's markets to a world-wide base. Sometimes creating a concise statement requires a little wordsmithing, but it's usually a straight forward process. The difficulty begins with selecting performance measures and deliverables.

In breakthrough plans, performance measures let you know when the objective is accomplished. In Rockford International's case, the number of countries where Rockford International products are sold is a good measure of how Rockford International is expanding its products into other countries. They started in 2005 selling in only one country. By 2010, Rockford International wants to be selling in at least twenty different countries. Since improvement in product quality is necessary to sell products through distributors, they also have a goal of reducing product returns from 0.5% in 2005 to less than 0.01% in 2010. These goals are clearly stretch goals. Rockford International may not know exactly how they will be achieved; however, the goals are based on expected future requirements and provide direction for resource and improvement activity selection. Improving quality and selling in multiple countries are noble goals, but if Rockford International does not also improve its business position what good will result? To assure balanced improvement Rockford International selected Revenue and Profit as counter balancing measures. The goals associated with these measures are not stretch goals. They can be thought of as "worst case" goals. The focus will be on the number of countries and product quality, but you don't want revenue and profit to degrade in the meantime.

By creating the top level objective and supporting performance measures and goals, Rockford International developed a tool to clearly identify its business direction and targets. The next step was to identify the essential strategies necessary to achieve its vision and long range objective. The situation analysis is again helpful. In Rockford International's case, a major strategy is to shift its marketing focus from direct sales to high volume dealers and distributors. This will require new processes to be developed and a new set of skills for its sales force. Product quality and reliability must be improved to meet dealer requirements. Shipping world wide will also require manufacturing process improvement. Due to high shipping cost and international regulations, Rockford International concluded that it will need to manufacture products in other countries. This will involve looking at the manufacturing process in a whole new light. The last key area Rockford International wanted to address was the work environment. The management team did not want to rush head long into expansion without making sure employees benefited from the process also. A senior manager accepted ownership for each key strategy and then identified performance measures and goals. This completed Rockford International's long range plan.

Long range plans don't need to be complicated. They often consist of just one planning table. It's rare to deploy long range plans more than one level. Deployment is limited, but the long range plan should be widely communicated. At each meeting when the

 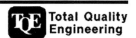

organization vision is discussed, managers should also discuss the overall objective and the strategies to achieve the objective. All employees do not need to have a copy of the long range plan, but because of its wide communication they know what the plan entails. When asked, they can articulate the plan's basic components.

Broad objectives help establish the organization direction. To make the long range plan a reality, however, specific steps must be taken this year. Those steps are documented in the annual plan.

Develop the Annual Plan

The annual plan describes the critical things that must be accomplished or implemented this year, in order for the organization to achieve its long range plan and vision. By shortening the planning window to one year, it's easier to determine what specific steps are required. Usually the problem is not identifying the steps; it's selecting which steps will be staffed. A common mistake new Hoshin users make is trying to accomplish too many objectives.

Annual Plan

➤ Specific steps of the Long Range plan to be accomplished this year.
➤ Deployed to all critical areas.
➤ Can change significantly from year to year.

Remember that business fundamentals must still be supported. The resources to accomplish breakthrough objectives are not free; but if the organization has done a good job of defining business fundamentals, about five to ten percent of the organization's resources should be available.

Hoshin uses the same form for the annual plan as it uses for the long range plan. Based on the long range plan, the organization identifies the most important steps to be accomplished this year. In the Rockford International example, to achieve its vision of being an international organization, the management team concluded that by the end of the first year they should be building products in at least one country other than the US. Refer to Rockford International's annual plan starting on page 110. Studying the present and future situation data, Rockford International selected Spain as their first international manufacturing location. Construction growth in Spain was impressive. Because of the 2006 World Games, Barcelona was experiencing exceptional growth. It just made sense for Rockford International management to make Barcelona, Spain their first step.

Notice how the situation statement on page 110 describes the same elements as the long range plan's situation but in a narrower, one year focus. After reading the annual plan's situation, it's obvious why the annual objective of shipping products from Rockford International's Barcelona plant is important. Notice that performance measures have goals set for a one year window. To achieve the objective of establishing a Barcelona

plant, the management team concluded that four key areas were important. They had to resolve all legal issues, locate and outfit a Spanish production facility, improve reliability of the parts to be built in Spain, and improve the organization's cost structure so they could make a profit. Owners were assigned and performance measures, deliverables, and goals defined. Notice that a mixture of performance measures and deliverables were selected to track progress.

Strategies should be selected to provide high confidence that the objective will be accomplished, but only the critical few strategies should be documented in the plan. Many people make the mistake of having too many strategies. This tends to dilute efforts to the point where very little progress is made on any strategy. Deploying numerous strategies can also become a paperwork nightmare. I recommend that no more than five strategies be documented. Typical Hoshin annual plans have only three or four strategies to accomplish each objective. Remember that the key words are "critical path" and "focus."

With the top planning table of the annual plan complete, each strategy owner treats their strategy as an objective and deploys it down one level. Breakthrough plans are not necessarily deployed along functional lines. They are often deployed cross functionally. Owners must be able to lead and coordinate resources that are outside of their control. The vision is clear and the key objectives are clear, but the impact on business fundamentals

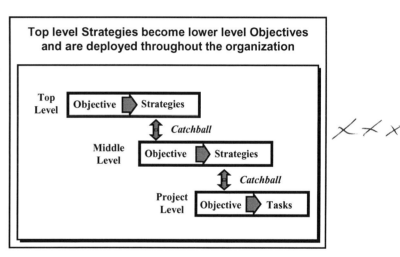

in other areas can be serious. To resolve these issues, catchball must be performed. As lower level strategies are developed, owners must continually test people's commitment to achieving breakthrough objectives and maintaining control of business fundamentals.

The objective to locate and outfit a Spanish production facility was accepted by the Manufacturing Manager, Chris Builder. This was a logical choice because of the expertise residing in the manufacturing function, but the owner could have been any member of the senior staff. On page 111, you see how Chris deployed that objective to the next lower level. Chris worked with her team to identify strategies necessary to accomplish the objective. They concluded the objective could be partitioned into three parallel strategies. One focus was to locate and outfit a production facility. Another focus was to hire and train Spanish workers. The third focus was to locate a Spanish supplier for the 15009 family of parts. Notice that only deliverables were selected to track progress. This is because each of the strategies could easily be described as a

project of individual tasks. The deliverables from the lower levels were rolled up this level.

You might ask what does locating a Spanish supplier have to do with outfitting a production facility. As it turns out, this strategy originally belonged to the Engineering Manager. When he evaluated Engineering's resource constraints with his team, they concluded they could not conduct design improvements and search for new suppliers at the same time. They proposed that since Chris' people would be in Spain anyway searching for a production facility, why couldn't they also search for a new supplier? The Materials department reported to Chris and had business fundamentals responsibility for supplier management. Pat Shepard, the Materials Manager, said she had available resources, so the objective was moved to Chris' annual plan. This example shows how the catchball process can work.

After identifying the three key strategies, Chris and her team selected deliverables for each strategy thus completing their planning table. On page 112, you can see how Pat Shepard deployed her objective down one more level. Notice that the form changed. This form is called an Implementation Plan. It's nothing more than a scheduled set of tasks. When the objective is clearly defined and everyone understands how it's to be accomplished, deployment using the standard planning table stops and this form is used. The guidelines for using an Implementation Plan are found on page 92. Feel free to use other schedule management tools in place of an Implementation Plan. The important thing to remember is that if a strategy is just a series of well understood, clearly defined tasks, then its time to shift from the planning table to the implementation plan[17] format.

By identifying the key objective for the annual plan and deploying it to all required areas, the organization has a focus for its breakthrough efforts. It's not necessary to deploy each strategy to everyone within the organization. Only critical path strategies should be deployed. This helps the periodic review process not waste time reviewing activities with little or no significant contribution to the key organization objectives. It's important for everyone to understand and contribute to the annual plan, but the Pareto principle should be applied to activities that are documented and reviewed. Failure to follow this guideline can create annual plans that are burdened with too much paperwork.

---

[17] In TQE's Hoshin software, the Implementation plan is not used. The software allows each Planning Table to be tracked using either or both performance measures and deliverables. Tracking a table using only deliverables will create a Gantt chart that looks very much like an Implementation plan.

 **Total Quality Engineering**

 Hoshin

The Plan Development Process

Hoshin plans are created on an annual cycle. Each year the management team begins a new planning cycle. Each organization has its own process that usually includes an off-site retreat. As I have already mentioned, I prefer to keep planning sessions on-site where more people can be involved and data can be accessed. The outline on the following page describes the process I prefer.

The first question you might ask is why I have a description of the mission and vision in the first step. Given that I previously stated in this chapter that the vision is created from an understanding of the business situation, how can it be the first step? The answer is simple. If you don't have a vision, you need data to create it, and it can't be the first step. If you already have a vision, it will not change much from year to year, and you want the vision to influence your data analysis. By reaffirming the mission, vision, and values in the first step, they can be used to evaluate effectiveness of potential alternatives.

The next steps collect and analyze data. The specific steps must be tailored to the organization's needs. Some organizations will not perform all steps and other organizations may need to add steps. I prefer to get as many people involved with these steps a possible. By assigning each data collection and analysis step to cross-functional teams, the collective wisdom of the organization can be leveraged. More importantly, the time people invest in creating the annual plan improves their buy-in and support. It becomes their plan instead of "stone tablets" handed down from senior management.

After SWOT analysis, it's senior management's responsibility to update the long range plan and define the key annual objective. The annual plan is then deployed using the catchball process.

Organization Plan Outline

1.0 Description of Mission, Vision (or strategic intent), Values and lessons learned from last year.

2.0 Description of current performance.
  2.1 Description of current sales by market segment.
  2.2 Description of competitors and their estimated sales by market segment.
  2.3 Description of distribution channels by market segment by supplier.
  2.4 Description of user needs by market segment.
  2.5 Description of customer satisfaction by user need by supplier.

3.0 Description of core competencies and how they address user needs.
  3.1 Description of core competencies (things you do very well).
  3.2 Description of core competency's applicability to new markets.
  3.3 Description of competitor's core competencies.
  3.4 Description of supplier's core competencies.

4.0 Description of internal and external forces impacting the future.
  4.1 Description of technology changes and implications.
  4.2 Description of predicted competitor moves and implications.
  4.3 Description of internal situation and implications.
  4.4 Description of supplier's future capabilities and implications.

5.0 Determine Strengths, Weaknesses, Opportunities and Threats (SWOT).
  5.1 Description of strengths that must be preserved.
  5.2 Description of weakness that must be improved.
  5.3 Description of threats (competitive, technological, etc.) that must be addressed.
  5.4 Description of opportunities to gain share and/or enter new markets

6.0 Long Range Plan: What things must be accomplished within three to five years?

7.0 Annual Plan: What things must be accomplished this year?

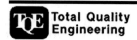

Department Specific Breakthroughs

The breakthrough planning process previously described was for organization-wide breakthroughs. Organization-wide breakthroughs are not necessarily deployed to everyone in the organization. It's possible that some departments will not have ownership of strategies that link directly to the organization-wide breakthrough[18]. For example, the Maintenance, Accounts Receivable, Employee Benefits, and Process Audit departments will probably not significantly contribute to a strategic breakthrough of entering a new market or developing a new technology. There is also the rare case of a department fully staffing its business fundamentals and its contribution to organization-wide breakthroughs and still have available resources. In either case the department should create a department specific breakthrough plan to implement process improvements directly relating to its key processes and core competencies.

Each department can be managed as if it's a small, independent organization. It has customers and processes to serve those customers. With a good business fundamentals plan, the department also has measures to track how well it's meeting customer requirements for delivery and quality, managing cost, and supporting its people. These measures make ideal sources for department specific breakthrough plans. Instead of the Maintenance department having token representation on the organization-wide objective to enter a new market, why not let them improve the hazardous waste disposal process? Rather than having the Accounts Receivable department have token representation on the organization-wide objective to develop a new technology, why not let them reduce the level of billing errors?

By allowing departments to pick breakthrough objectives intended to improve their own processes, you run the risk of diluting the organization focus. To keep department specific breakthroughs focused in the right direction, make sure everyone understands the organization-wide objectives. It's desirable to have all department specific breakthroughs relate to organization-wide objectives; but they definitely should not be in conflict with organization-wide objectives.

Department specific breakthroughs are documented in Hoshin just like organization-wide breakthroughs. The same forms are used. The situation statement is an excellent place to document the rationalization for selecting a department specific objective over direct support of organization-wide breakthroughs.

---

[18] Not all Hoshin experts agree with me on this point. Some advocate that organization strategic initiatives be broad enough to allow everyone in the organization to contribute. For example, if the strategic initiative is "reduce cost" then everyone can create cost reduction objectives that link directly to the organization objective. I believe that in some situations this technique is appropriate. On the other hand, when the strategic initiative is focused, like entering new markets or developing new technology, it's very difficult to find meaningful contributions for everyone. I have found that trying to do so trivializes the process and prevents people from staffing department specific breakthroughs that could really be significant.

Completing the Plan

At this point in the process, every organizational unit within the organization should have a business fundamentals plan. The plan should document why the unit exists and how it supports the organization's mission. The plan should identify the people responsible for each activity and measures to track performance.

Everyone should also understand and be aware of the organization's long range plan. Each organizational unit within the organization should have an annual plan that is consistent with the long range plan. The annual plan should identify how the unit will change its business fundamentals to meet future needs. If unit resources are critical to achieving organization-wide breakthrough objectives, then the unit's annual plan should directly link to the organization-wide objective through the deployment process. If the unit's resources are not critical to achieving the organization-wide objective, then the unit's annual plan should address improving key success factors relating to the unit's unique situation.

By completing these plans, everyone will know what must be accomplished for the organization to be successful both today and tomorrow. They can now begin working the plan. This leads us to the next step in the Hoshin process: periodic reviews.

Chapter 6

Periodic Review

Are we on track? Do we need to make adjustments? What have we learned?

Setting Expectations of Performance

People work on things that are important. Management determines what is important by the questions they ask and the things they check. If a great plan is created and management never checks to see how the plan is progressing, you can rest assured that the plan will sit on the shelf and not be used to manage the business. If management does not check the plan's status, then the plan is not important!

To make the Hoshin plan important, management must periodically check on how well the plan is progressing. Hoshin periodic reviews stress the importance of the plan and set expectations for performance. The flowchart on page 68 shows the Hoshin annual planning cycle. Notice how the planning cycle is based on the PDCA process. The *Plan* step was described in the previous three chapters. The *Do* step is self-explanatory, that is, work the plan. The *Check* and *Act* steps are implemented by Hoshin periodic reviews.

In general and especially if you are just starting to use Hoshin, periodic reviews should be conducted monthly. Reviews for higher levels of management can be reduced to quarterly as you become comfortable with Hoshin. All management levels should conduct an annual review of how well the plan was implemented.

Periodic reviews should critically compare expected results to actual results. The root cause of all deviations from expectations should be understood. Based on the learning experience, expectations for the next review period should be modified. When objectives are achieved, all gains should be standardized to prevent backsliding.

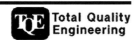

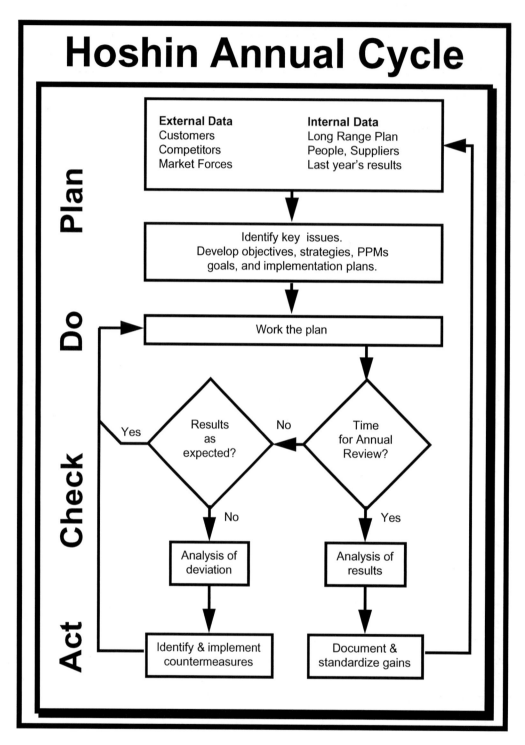

Hoshin Annual Cycle

Plan

External Data	Internal Data
Customers	Long Range Plan
Competitors	People, Suppliers
Market Forces	Last year's results

Identify key issues.
Develop objectives, strategies, PPMs
goals, and implementation plans.

Do

Work the plan

Check

Yes — Results as expected? — No — Time for Annual Review?

No — Analysis of deviation

Yes — Analysis of results

Act

Identify & implement countermeasures

Document & standardize gains

Adapted from the Hewlett-Packard model

The Review Process

Effective reviews are scheduled. A Planning Calendar is a good way to document when reviews will occur. People need to know that reviews will always occur and that they are expected to participate. The old adage, "You inspect what you expect" holds true. If management does not demonstrate that they value the review process, then employees will not value it either. Infrequent reviews or reviews that just gloss over the issues imply that the things being reviewed are not important. Nobody wants to work on something that's not important.

Effective reviews meet the following characteristics:

- Conducted on a regular basis.

- Come as you are. Fancy presentations are not required.

- Use actual performance data, not opinions or anecdotes.

- An open, honest and supportive atmosphere is maintained.

- Review business fundamentals first, followed by status of breakthrough activities.

The need for regular reviews was already discussed, but conducting the review should not be a lot of work. The Hoshin Periodic Review Table and Review Table Summary forms are used to facilitate the review process. Examples of these forms and rules for their use are found on pages 94 through 97. The forms utilize the PDCA cycle to compare actual results to expected results. The Review Table Summary is useful for documenting numerous activities on one page, but has the limitation of not providing much room for descriptive analysis. The Periodic Review Table documents status of one activity and provides room for descriptive analysis. The choice of which form to use is left to the user. I recommend Review Table Summaries be used for business fundamentals and management summaries of breakthrough activities. For review of a specific breakthrough activity, I recommend the Periodic Review Table. It provides a much better audit trail of activity[19].

It's important for reviews to include data. It's very easy to make statements like "made progress" or "will continue efforts." If these statements are made on reviews, you will find they tend to show up on every review and there will be little evidence of real progress. Quantifying progress using real data helps focus on real issues. It forces the question, "Why was the goal not achieved?" The discussion that follows provides insight into issues and helps identify alternatives for improvement.

---

[19] TQE's Hoshin software only implements the detailed Periodic Review Table, but summary reports of detailed review tables can be printed that provide the same functionality as the Review Table Summary form. See pages 129 and 130 in the Great Northern example plan.

Hoshin

Total Quality Engineering

When conducting the review, it's important for the manager to maintain a calm, non-threatening attitude. Attacking the process owner every time goals are not met will cause the process owner to cover up or omit negative information. This will destroy the review process. It's the manager's responsibility to assure an open, honest and supportive environment. This environment is critical.

In Hoshin reviews, the table owner brings all completed review forms and supporting data to the review meeting. Business fundamentals are reviewed first. Generally they will be performing to expectations, and therefore this part of the review should be very quick. There is no need to spend a lot of time on things that are working as expected. Just flashing the performance measure graphs is usually all that needs to be done. However, if one or more performance measures exceeded their action limits during the review period, the owner should describe the issue and the action taken to resolve and prevent its reoccurrence. An Abnormality Table is useful to document the deviation and corrective action. An Abnormality Table and guidelines for its use are found on pages 102 and 103.

After reviewing business fundamentals, attention should shift to breakthrough objectives. The table owner uses a completed Review Table to share the status of objectives. The reviewing manager should ask questions to assure that the root cause of all deviations from plan is understood. Catchball should occur between the reviewing manager and the table owner to reach agreement on the "Expected result next period." If expected results are too ambitious, motivation will be degraded because the owner will be unable to achieve them. On the other hand, if expected results are not challenging, it will not motivate exceptional performance. The "Expected result next period" section should document activities that can reasonably be accomplished during the next review period.

As the year progresses, it may become obvious that the original objective will not be achieved. This could be due to changes in the organization's situation that require a change in plans or the fact that resources were underestimated. If this happens, the Review Table can be used to document the changes without recreating the annual plan. Expected results should be updated as required to reflect the changes. There is no need to continue to hold owners accountable for results that everyone agrees will not be met.

To illustrate the review process, I'll use the Rockford International example again. On page 112 is the Implementation Plan to select a Spanish source for the 15009 family of parts. Remember that this activity was mandated by the Spanish government, (refer to the Situation Statement on page 111). Pat Shepard has ownership for this objective. The Implementation Plan breaks the objective into smaller tasks. Each task is owned by an employee in Pat's department. Notice that in January two tasks were expected to be completed; research alternatives and mail interest letters. Both tasks were owned by Tom Terrific.

Pat Shepard established regular reviews on the first Tuesday of each month. On the first Tuesday of February, 2005, Pat met with her team to review January performance. Business fundamentals were discussed first. Pat displayed the Department's Business Fundamentals Review Summary. Refer to form on page 116[20]. Pat pointed out that all performance measures were within limits except for "Time to Close Issues." It had exceeded its action limit due to a problem with the 37508 parts. Pat was already aware of the problem because Tom Terrific immediately notified her when the action limit was exceeded. During the review, Pat questioned Tom regarding the status of resolving the problem and preventing its reoccurrence.

Tom Terrific used an Abnormality Table to share the status. The report is found on page 117. At the time of the February review, only the top two blocks were completed. Tom explained how the problem was exposed in production and that he now understood the root cause. He was working with the supplier, but they had not determined a way to restart production. This issue would continue to be his top priority. Pat asked Tom if he needed additional resources to resolve the issue. Tom responded that he felt confident he could handle it himself. Pat agreed with Tom's action plan and turned her attention to breakthrough activity.

Tom Terrific was again the focus of the discussion because he had responsibility for the breakthrough deliverables due in January. Tom shared the Review Table shown on page 113. He noted that his research of potential suppliers was complete, but the interest letters had not been mailed. He said that he could still meet the schedule and that everything was on track. When Tom originally presented this table, the lessons learned section was blank. Pat did not share Tom's confidence that everything was on track. She pointed out that starting the Barcelona production facility was very critical to Rockford International's long range plan and that it must stay on schedule. Pat and her team discussed various options and agreed to a contingency plan of having Elaine pick up responsibility for mailing the letters if Tom could not resolve the 37508 problem within one week. They documented the contingency plan on Tom's Review Table in the "lessons learned" section.

On the first Tuesday in March, Pat held her regularly scheduled review meeting. By this time, all business fundamentals were within their action limits. Tom shared the completed Abnormality Report shown on page 117. Pat complimented Tom on a job well done. The team then turned their attention to breakthrough status, and Tom shared the Review Table shown on page 114. Interest letters were mailed, but no replies had been received. Tom believed this was understandable due to the late mailing date. He also pointed out that he had learned a valuable lesson regarding communication with Spain. In the future, he would use the fax machine instead of relying on the Spanish

---

[20] This form is actually a quarterly summary, but it would have looked very much the same during Pat's February review of performance.

Hoshin

Total Quality Engineering

postal service. Pat had some concerns, but given the alternatives she concluded the current plan was the best course of action.

On the first Tuesday in April, Pat held her regularly scheduled review meeting. Business fundamentals continued to remain within their action limits. Tom shared his Review Table (page 115). He pointed out that everything was on schedule. Fifteen requests for bid letters were faxed, and he was renewing his passport in preparation for site visits. Pat agreed with Tom's assessment and complimented him on a job well done.

After completing her department reviews, Pat worked with her boss, Chris Builder, and the rest of Chris' staff to create the first quarter review of Operation's breakthrough objectives. The Review Tables they created are shown on pages 118 and 119. Notice that the table on page 118 documents the status of Q1 activity. They also completed the first column of the Q2 review form. Completing the Expected Results column for the next review at the same time the current review is conducted prevents objectives from creeping during the next review period.

Annual Reviews

Monthly reviews tend to be working sessions. They are action oriented and results focused. At least once a year, however, you should reflect on the whole year's progress. This is called the annual review. The annual review is the start of the next year's planning process. I prefer to conduct annual reviews off-site. Get away from the day to day pressure and spend time critically analyzing the impact of your action and results.

The first part of the annual review should allow each objective owner to share an overview of their activity and results. Since some objectives are deployed throughout the organization, you might want to consider a team approach to the presentations. Each presentation should not be more than fifteen minutes. It should highlight the key objectives and results. Most importantly, the presentations should describe what was learned during the year and how that learning impacts the direction of the long range plan or how it could be leveraged into other areas. There should be little comment during the presentations. The intent is to let everyone else know what happened and what the group learned.

After the individual presentations, I like to form small groups to discuss, clarify and summarize the key lessons learned during the past year. The primary deliverable of each group is to recommend how the long range plan should be adjusted and what priorities exist for next year's annual plan. This information will trigger next year's annual planning process.

I like to conclude the annual review with a celebration. It's an excellent time to recognize and show appreciation for people's hard work. Have some fun. Enjoy a good meal. Shake everyone's hand and say thank you.

Standardizing Gains

As you conduct reviews, there will be times when the objective is achieved. The last thing you want is to repeat the same improvement effort a year from now. Too often, improvements are lost because new processes are not standardized.

Gains are standardized by moving breakthrough improvements into business fundamentals. Remember that business fundamentals are characterized by processes that are operating normally. They are documented, well understood, and include a balanced set of performance measures and action limits. If a process is not capable of meeting *desired* performance, then breakthrough effort is required to change the process so it will be capable. After the new process has been piloted and tested, people should be trained in the new process and process documentation should be updated. Assuming you have already seen improvement in the performance measures, you should also update the action limits to reflect the new *normal* performance.

Some breakthroughs actually eliminate the need for some business fundamental activities. If this happens, they should be removed from the appropriate Business Fundamental Planning Tables and resources reassigned. Other breakthrough efforts will create a new process. This creates a business fundamental that did not previously exist. You must determine which Business Fundamental Planning Table will pick up the new activity and adjust resources as required.

Recognize that every breakthrough objective will create, eliminate, or improve a business fundamental process. By making sure that all breakthroughs are ultimately standardized on a Business Fundamentals Planning Table, you will assure that gains will not be lost.

Planning Calendar

One of the best ways to assure that Hoshin is implemented correctly is to establish a planning calendar. The planning calendar describes the sequence of activities necessary to orchestrate the planning process. It also defines when information necessary for plan development will be collected. A typical planning calendar is shown below:

January	Monthly review of business fundamentals and breakthroughs.
February	Monthly review of business fundamentals and breakthroughs.
March	Monthly review of business fundamentals and breakthroughs. Q1 review of organization business fundamentals and breakthroughs.
April	Monthly review of business fundamentals and breakthroughs. Conduct employee morale survey.
May	Monthly review of business fundamentals and breakthroughs.
June	Monthly review of business fundamentals and breakthroughs. Q2 review of organization business fundamentals and breakthroughs.
July	Monthly review of business fundamentals and breakthroughs. Complete competitive product analysis process.
August	Monthly review of business fundamentals and breakthroughs. Complete customer satisfaction analysis process.
September	Monthly review of business fundamentals and breakthroughs. Q3 review of organization business fundamentals and breakthroughs.
October	Monthly review of business fundamentals and breakthroughs. Conduct customer visits. Conduct employee morale survey.
November	Monthly review of business fundamentals and breakthroughs. Receive and review corporate Hoshin objectives.
December	Monthly review of business fundamentals and breakthroughs. Annual review of all business fundamentals and breakthroughs. Develop and distribute Hoshin plan for next year.

A Hoshin Implementation Plan is another useful way to document the planning calendar. The format is not important. What is important is scheduling meetings to review the results of each activity and establishing the discipline to complete each step. If specific dates are not established, the probability of success is significantly reduced.

Chapter 7

Barriers, Mistakes, and Implementation Tips

All this sounds great, but how do I implement Hoshin in my organization?

Finding Motivation for Change

If things are going well with your organization, you're probably not motivated to make changes. Many US managers still subscribe to the philosophy of "If it's not broke, don't fix it." The problem with that philosophy is that in today's dynamic times stable performance is usually left behind. Competition has never been more intense than it is today. Fear of competitive threats is the first motivator for organizational change.

The second motivator is dissatisfaction with the current process. If you are frustrated with your rate of progress, if you are looking for a way to communicate organization policy to all employees, if you want to empower employees to assume more responsibility, if your organization has difficulty getting big jobs completed because of constant fire fighting, if you want to implement a Total Quality Management culture within your organization, then Hoshin may be just the tool you need. Be warned; Hoshin is not a quick fix. Successful Hoshin implementation, just like any major organizational change, requires a change in the culture of the organization. Changing culture is similar to weight control. Fad diets generate quick, visible results, but most weight is quickly regained. The experts agree; the only long term solution to weight control is life-style change. The only way to truly implement Hoshin is to change the way you manage.

The third motivation for change is a genuine desire for constant improvement. This motivation is usually precipitated by a combination of the first two, but unlike fear and

frustration the desire for constant improvement is never satisfied. Once you are driven by the desire to always make things better, your organization's culture will have truly changed.

First Steps

After you decide to implement Hoshin, the first question is where to start? Most people jump right into deploying a large number of objectives throughout the organization. This has a tendency to overwhelm employees, and they view it as a "flavor of the month" program. If they don't take active steps to undermine and destroy your efforts, they will maliciously comply with the "letter of the law" but not change what they are doing. Employees know that if they just wait long enough, you will get tired and forget the whole thing.

The problem with this approach is that focusing on breakthrough activities without first establishing a firm foundation of business fundamentals is just "more stuff to do." Employees become confused about what's important. They hear management cheerleading Hoshin, but they know if shipments are not met, there is going to be trouble. To use a football analogy, it's like teaching the double reverse play before players know how to block and tackle.

My experience has shown that most negative impressions of Hoshin have come from people that have tried to implement it in a quick fix manner. They make comments like, "We tried it for three months, and it didn't work for us." Remember that changing culture takes time. Although tangible benefits can be attained in months, it often takes years before the full impact of Hoshin can be realized.

Assuming you have avoided the first typical mistake, I recommend the following sequential steps for Hoshin implementation:

1. Define missions
2. Define values
3. Select performance measures and compute action limits
4. Begin periodic review
5. Define vision
6. Begin annual breakthrough planning cycle

To support Hoshin implementation, I suggest that you set proper expectations. By that I mean establish the expectation that *you* are going to use Hoshin. If your personal commitment is not demonstrated, your effort will have a poor chance of success. Most importantly, do not delegate Hoshin implementation to others while your own processes remain unchanged. Hoshin implementation begins with you!

Get started, but go slow. Don't try to implement all components at once and deploy to 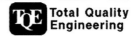 everyone. If you manage a large organization, it's best to just work with your staff first. Once they are comfortable with the process, deploy it to the next level of management. If you are nervous that starting at the top of a large organization could become difficult, then find a smaller group with a leader that understands and is excited about Hoshin. Let this group act as a pilot for the organization. Starting small allows Hoshin to be tailored to the organization's culture.

I recommend that you train people as you go instead of relying on mass training. I have heard mass training described as drinking from a fire hose. It's difficult to absorb everything. More is retained if training is provided just prior to when it's needed. I suggest the Learn-Use-Teach-Inspect method. LUTI begins when a small group Learns Hoshin concepts. They Use Hoshin in order to become familiar with it and then Teach it to others (usually their subordinates). After teaching, they Inspect to assure the concepts are being used correctly. LUTI continues with students becoming teachers and training others until everyone is trained. The concept of inspection is very important. As I mentioned earlier, reviewing progress is critical to effective implementation. If you preach Hoshin but only inspect to see if daily shipments are being made, people will quickly learn that shipments are important and you work on Hoshin if you have time. Establishing the expectation that Hoshin is the way daily shipments are tracked reinforces the Hoshin process without losing sight of the fact that shipments are important.

Large Organizations - Loose Linkage

The ideal organization for Hoshin implementation is a small to midsize organization focused on a single mission. This can range from a one-person consulting firm to an organization with about 2000 people. While the organization will often have world-wide sales and support people, the bulk of the people work at a central location. There is one senior manager (e.g., CEO, President, General Manager, Region Manager, District Manager, or Division Head). The organization is focused on a specific product family, geographic region, or customer segment. The organization has profit and loss responsibility or expense control for its area of focus.

Since the vast majority of organizations fit the above description, Hoshin implementation in most organizations will look very similar to the examples in Chapter 8. Implementing Hoshin in large, multinational organizations, however, can be a little more difficult. Most of the Hoshin early adopters in the US were large organizations like Hewlett-Packard and Xerox, but they all started by piloting the process in self-contained divisions. Each of these small entities fit the description of the ideal organization. As Hoshin spread, there was the need to align the individual entity Hoshin plans with the corporate Hoshin plan. Hewlett-Packard initially tried to create one Hoshin plan for the entire organization, but that effort quickly failed as the plan became so large that it died of its own weight. In addition, improvement strategies tended to be generic and as a result, a lot of important effort was not captured by the plan. Based on my discussions with Hoshin implementers at Xerox, they also concluded that one Hoshin plan for the entire organization was unworkable. We solved the problem at Hewlett-Packard by using the concept of "loose linkage."

Loose linkage means that each entity has its own Hoshin plan that is loosely linked to the Hoshin plan of its parent entity. Loose linkage implies that there is not necessarily one-to-one deployment of strategies of the parent entity to lower level entities. For example, assume the corporate Hoshin plan includes strategies for improving customer satisfaction and reducing cost. Assume there are eight business segments in the corporation. With loose linkage each business segment is free to decide which corporate strategies they will support in their annual plan in addition to entity specific strategies. For example, segment one might have issues with both customer satisfaction and cost, and as a result will develop strategies in both corporate focus areas. On the other hand, maybe business segment two already leads the corporation in customer satisfaction so it will develop strategies in the areas of cost reduction and market penetration.

The intent of loose linkage is to provide a guide for lower level Hoshin plan development but not impose strict adherence to higher level strategies. Loose linkage prevents a strategy that is valid at the corporate level from forcing a lower entity to consume resources on something that has a low priority for its specific situation. Obviously the improved flexibility of loose linkage allows for a dilution of focus and even abuse, so rigorous catchball is required. When implemented correctly, loose linkage aligns Hoshin plans throughout the organization and provides flexibility for individual entities to use their resources in the most effective manner.

Tracking Hoshin Implementation

One of the best ways to implement Hoshin Kanri is to include its implementation in your organization's Hoshin plan. In other words, you create a Hoshin plan to implement Hoshin. Since Hoshin is data driven you will need a way to track your implementation. A technique that I have found helpful is to create a Hoshin Maturity Score. Since all organizations are different, I rarely use the same maturity criteria. The criteria are defined based on the unique needs of each organization. In general, however, there are common elements of all Hoshin implementations.

The ultimate goal is to have Hoshin become the way the organization is managed. If that is the case, then the maturity criteria should work backwards from that goal defining a series of steps leading up to the goal. I have documented typical maturity criteria in Appendix E and there is a sample MS Excel spreadsheet used to compute the maturity score on the CD. By measuring Hoshin maturity once each month, you will have a better picture of how well your Hoshin implementation is proceeding.

Overcoming Barriers

As with any change, new process pioneers must overcome barriers. Hoshin is no exception. In addition to the normal resistance to change, Hoshin has some specific barriers that must be overcome. The first is its name.

Because of Hoshin's Japanese origins, some people are reluctant to use it because of the Japanese name. I suspect that's why some US organizations use *Policy Deployment* as the name. Unfortunately, I have not found an English translation of *hoshin kanri* that captures all of the Japanese meanings. Each translation leaves out some key element. For example, Policy Deployment captures the essence of deploying breakthrough plans and as a result people fail to use Hoshin for business fundamentals.

During my implementation of Hoshin at HP, people suggested that the name be changed to something less Japanese. I resisted because I felt we were spending too much time on positioning and not enough time on understanding the Hoshin process. I had a similar experience with the name syndrome as a rookie youth soccer coach. I was in a large coach's meeting where the president of the club passed around a list and asked us to select a team name and colors. He cautioned us to make sure we did not repeat a name or colors that had already been selected. He then started the list on the other side of the room. I turned to the coach next to me and said, "Great! By the time the list gets to us, the only colors left will be black and blue." As the words left my mouth, I had a brainstorm. Why not call the team the Bruisers with colors of black and blue?

At the first team meeting, I introduced myself and announced that the team name was the Bruisers. The reaction of the fourteen, nine year old boys was scary. They made gagging sounds, and demanded that I change the name. I am not sure why I resisted. Maybe I was too enamored with my own "clever thinking," but I stood firm. I said, "Listen guys, it doesn't matter what you are called. If you win, people will name their kids after the Bruisers." As it turned out, the Bruisers were a pretty good team. They played for the county championship. Unfortunately, they lost by a score of 2 to 1, but no one ever made fun of the Bruiser name. I received a lot of calls from parents that wanted their boy to be a Bruiser.

I guess the moral of the story is to not become distracted over name debates. If you must change the name, then do it but do it quickly. I call the process "Hoshin."

The next barrier to action is perceived lack of top management support. People ask how can they implement Hoshin if their top management isn't bought in. I agree that if top management is committed to Hoshin, then implementation is a whole lot easier; but I do not believe that top management commitment is a prerequisite for getting started. You are the "top management" of everything you manage. If you believe Hoshin can help you manage more effectively then why do you need to wait for direction from above?

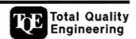

Implement Hoshin in your own part of the organization. You can take advantage of Hoshin even if you are an individual contributor. Many independent consultants use Hoshin to manage their efforts. Successful Hoshin implementation generally yields improved performance. Your "best practice" example will then be copied by others wanting the same success. Top management will soon become very interested in Hoshin. The bottom line is, don't wait until everyone is bought in before you take action. Become a **pocket of excellence** yourself.

Hoshin is driven by measures, but sometimes employees fear measures will be used against them. This is especially true if there is a history of mutual disrespect between management and employees. As long as accountability is vague and there are no measures of performance, then blame is diluted and people feel safe in the crowd. I like to respond to this barrier with, "Yes! Your performance will be measured and you will be held accountable for successful performance. However, I will make sure we both agree on your objectives and as long as you perform to the best of your ability, you will not be punished for failure to meet the objectives." This statement establishes an expectation of performance but does so in a safe environment. Employees must feel that it's OK to fail. Willful misconduct or gross negligence can't be tolerated; but as long as people are doing the best job they know how to do and are learning and improving with each mistake, then what more can be asked?

Because of the tops down nature of Hoshin deployment, some people feel that creativity will be stifled. If plans are deployed in a dictatorial manner, this fear will be realized. People will learn to only do as they are told. On the other hand, if care is taken to assure people understand not only the specific steps of their job but also the underlying intent and if breakthrough objectives are deployed with effective catchball then creativity is not stifled, it's enhanced and focused. Hoshin acts to focus creativity on the critical few issues and not waste it on the less important many.

The final barrier is often the toughest. People perceive that Hoshin requires too much paperwork and overhead. If you fall victim to some of the common mistakes listed in the next section, Hoshin can become a paperwork jungle. By following some simple techniques, however, the paperwork can be significantly reduced. A typical department's Hoshin plan can consist of less than twelve pages, including one page for business fundamentals, one page for the organization's long range plan, one to five pages for the department's portion of the annual plan, and four quarterly review summaries. I have never found it necessary for everyone to have a complete plan including every other department's planning tables. In a large organization, this could be a very thick document. If you still feel the need to do so, I suggest that only one or two master copies be kept. Do not distribute the entire compilation to everyone. Communicate the overall organization direction through organization wide presentations and/or newsletters, but keep individual department Hoshin plans simple.

Another solution to the paperwork issue is Hoshin software. After hearing complaints about too much paperwork, I created software to facilitate the process. You can learn more about the software in Appendix D. The example plans for Great Northern (page 120) were created using the software.

Common Mistakes

During implementation of any new process you are bound to make a few mistakes. I have made or observed almost every major Hoshin implementation mistake. I hope you can learn from my mistakes so your implementation will be easier.

Lack of Periodic Review

I have already mentioned the importance of management's involvement with periodic reviews, but I cannot over emphasize this point. The primary reason Hoshin is not used to manage the organization is because managers drop the ball! Many managers do a very good job establishing their vision, mission, and values; but then they never check to see if it made a difference. They allow themselves to be diverted into firefight mode and fail to observe the big picture of how the organization is functioning. Most managers are good fire fighters. That's usually why they were promoted in the first place. They are comfortable solving problems, and they receive a sense of job satisfaction from it. Unfortunately, this activity prevents them from doing their most important job; providing leadership for the organization. Managers must stop playing the game and start coaching the players.

The performance expectations managers set, the questions they ask, and the things they check determine what's important. In my use of Hoshin, I learned that periodic reviews are one of my best tools to influence employee behavior. I use reviews to set the tone for organization performance. Reviews give me an opportunity to share my expectations, collect input, and build consensus on action. In short, reviews help me build a functioning team.

The first problem I had with reviews was determining when to conduct them. There always seemed to be a good reason to delay or cancel a review. If a few key managers were out of town, customers were visiting, or there was a conflict with another meeting, the Hoshin periodic review meeting would be canceled. At one point, I noticed that we had not conducted a review in three months and it seemed our Hoshin plan had turned into a "wish-list" document. We were not using the plan to guide our activities. I concluded that I was setting the wrong expectations.

To change our behavior, I changed the process. I had a regularly scheduled staff meeting each Thursday. I selected the staff meeting on the second Thursday of each month as our Hoshin review meeting. Everyone knew when the meeting was to be held, and they were expected to manage their schedules to not conflict with the review meeting. There would always be reasons why a manager might miss a meeting every now and then, but they were required to send a substitute if they couldn't attend. If a manager consistently sent a substitute to the meeting, I conducted a "career counseling" session with that manager. I asked the manager why he/she felt it was not important to fulfill his/her management responsibilities. The bottom line was the meetings would always be held -- they would never be canceled!

I characterize my first review as a "milk-toast" or "feel good" meeting. Managers presented anecdotal evidence that everything was fine. I asked probing questions during each presentation and quickly exposed that very little had actually been accomplished. I asked for data and they had none to share. My questions embarrassed many of my managers, but it changed the flavor of our next review meeting.

The second review had much more use of data, but progress was still lagging and excuses were plentiful. The excuses usually involved a lack of resources. I asked probing questions and found that some managers were staffing low priority activities and not staffing critical breakthrough objectives. I gave them permission to stop supporting the low priority activities and "suggested" they shift the resources to the critical breakthroughs. I also learned that some managers had really accepted more responsibility than they could handle. For these managers I eliminated or transferred responsibility for some of their activities so they could focus on the critical areas.

By conducting reviews on a regular basis and shifting resources to assure the critical activities were staffed I set an expectation for acceptable performance. It was not long before the new behaviors became part of all meetings. I realized that the review process had actually changed the way we managed. The plan had become the tool that focused our action instead of a document that collected dust on the shelf.

 Too Many Strategies

Probably the most frequent mistake is trying to accomplish too many things at once. It's common for new users to have annual plans with over ten strategies for each objective. The obvious problem is that it's difficult to manage that many items in a structured manner. It also creates a paperwork jungle. I suggest you let good judgment prevail. Document and manage only the critical few items. Let some of the lower priority activities run on automatic. Sometimes when lower level activities are not managed closely, they tend to disappear. Obviously, if that happens, you didn't need to manage them in the first place. If they will not go away, then you will have more information to

properly determine their priority. The rule I follow is to only have three to five strategies for any breakthrough objective.

A prime reason people generate too many strategies is that they document events as strategies. For example, suppose the objective is to "Install new computers." To achieve the objective the following strategies are created: 1) purchase computers, 2) setup hardware, 3) install software, and 4) train users. Each of these strategies can be described as an event. Nothing happens until its time and after the strategy is completed no effort is devoted to the strategy. Documenting the effort as a strategy creates a planning table that must be reviewed on a periodic basis. This ends up complicating the plan in order to document a simple task. A better approach is to document the above "strategies" as "deliverables". That way you don't create additional planning tables and require reviews to be conducted when nothing is scheduled to happen. The rule I follow is to never create a strategy when a deliverable will do. Following this rule will greatly simplify your Hoshin plan.

Analysis Paralysis

Hoshin requires rigorous use of data and data analysis. People want the plan to be perfect so there is always the tendency to want more data. This can add delay to the planning process and in some cases even cause it to stop.

The best way to prevent analysis paralysis is recognize that you don't need a perfect plan to move forward. I have never fully executed a Hoshin plan from start to finish exactly as it was originally planned. Something always came up that caused the plan to change. Hoshin uses the review process to manage changes to the plan. Lessons learned and new data are integrated into periodic review so that the plan adjusts to new situations.

I don't mean to imply that you should not collect and analyze data in order to create a good plan. Effective planning can prevent huge blunders down the line, but how do you know when to stop planning and enter the Do phase. I use the "reasonable confidence" test. When you have reasonable confidence that the objective is achievable you can then exit the planning phase and count on the Hoshin review process to handle changes to the plan.

Too focused on structure

Hoshin is based on specific forms and rules for their use. Sometimes, people get so wrapped up in the form structure making sure that each "t" is crossed and each "i" dotted that they forget the overall objective. They debate terminology and whether an item belongs in the annual plan or business fundamentals.

An over emphasis on structure can cause people to loose sight of the big picture. The best way to overcome this mistake is to break the rules every now and then. Recognize that Hoshin rules provide a framework for structured thinking, but you are not going to be arrested if you bend a rule. The review process will provide clues to whether or not bending the rule was a good idea. This technique allows the organization to modify Hoshin to better fit its planning needs.

Performance Measure Misuse

Many people have a hard time selecting measures that truly track performance. This is an especially big problem with a manual or paper form driven Hoshin process. It's easy for people to include a measure on a planning table without having a data collection process in place. Without data, you can't have a performance measure. Anytime someone says they use a measure, I ask to see the graph. If the graph does not exist, then they don't have a performance measure. Using TQE's Hoshin software eliminates this mistake because it forces the use of graphical data.

Assuming graphs do exist, the next problem is that the measures focus only on one aspect. For example, in my Hoshin consulting work I find senior management have plenty of financial measures but few measures to show if customers are satisfied, employees are properly trained, or if the distribution channel is effective. The lack of a balanced set of performance measures creates situations were one measure is optimized at the expense of other measures.

One of the main premises of the Balanced Scorecard (Appendix A) is that financial performance is not the only measure of organization success. Of course financial performance is important, but it's almost impossible to manage by just looking at the bottom line. If that's all you monitored there would only be two modes of management: "everything's great" or "Alarm! Alarm!"

The way I attempt to correct this mistake is to require that a set of four balanced measures be selected for each planning table. One measure selected in each the areas of quality, cost, delivery, and people. After there is sufficient data, an analysis can be performed to see if measures provide insight into organization performance. If not, then we modify, drop, and/or add measures.

Spend time training on the basic concepts of process management and process variation. Let people select any measure; but ask probing questions during reviews to expose the measure's strengths and weaknesses. Allow them to execute a PDCA cycle to come up with better measures.

By far, the biggest misuse of performance measures is treating goals like action limits. During the annual planning process a measure like Customer Satisfaction will be selected for improvement. The baseline and goal values are established and then a linear extrapolation between the two end points will become the "monthly target" for Customer Satisfaction. Now each month, management wants to know if the improvement is on target and if not why. Unfortunately, because people know they must have answers, they make stuff up. It's all smoke and mirrors which ends up actually taking away from true improvement.

The problem is that improvements are practically never achieved in a linear manner. Improvements are made in step functions. Some steps are big but most are small. The combined effect of many step improvements may show linear growth, but often it does not. Demanding adherence to short term linear growth really means management does not understand the improvement process. It's far better to ignore the goal and focus on the implementation schedule of the process improvement effort until that effort is complete. You complete the PDCA cycle by determining if the improvement achieved the desired impact on the measure.

Effective use of performance measures requires constant coaching. About the best recommendation I can provide is to recognize that the weakness exists and be prepared to question, teach, coach, and encourage.

Plan Security

Many organizations treat their strategic plan as a top secret document -- so secret that employees don't know what it is. It's generally not a good idea to freely share your organization plans with your competitors, but it helps if employees know what's going on. Situations exist that do require plan secrecy; but in the vast majority of cases I believe the security fear is unfounded. You have to trust employees to keep the best interest of the organization in mind. Tell them that the plan is for internal use only and is not to be disclosed to non-employees. If they do not know the plan's objectives, how can you expect them to act responsibly and creatively to accomplish the plan?

In most cases, you do not need to worry about outsiders getting knowledge of your plans. They probably will not act on it anyway. Effective planning processes are not characterized by elaborate, detailed plans. They are characterized by *excellence in execution*. I am reminded of a high school football coach's comments. He drilled us on executing plays perfectly. He told us that he wanted us to execute so well that we could

walk up to the line of scrimmage, shout the play out loud so the other team knew what we were going to do, and still gain five yards. By practicing *excellence in execution* you will not have to worry about your competition. Once you decide what you want to do, they will not be able to stop you.

Linking Hoshin to Employee Compensation

This is a very complex subject. I don't want to imply that it's a mistake to link employee compensation and/or bonus performance to the Hoshin plan, but I have never seen it done very well. In just about every organization that I've introduced to Hoshin, the HR manager proposes that the Hoshin plan become the prime vehicle to manage employee performance evaluations and determine compensation. They visualize the Hoshin plan being deployed to every employee so individual performance is quantified and individual results can be directly translated into compensation.

In theory, the Hoshin process can support this concept, but there are many pitfalls and problems with the approach. The first is that Hoshin Kanri was not designed to be an employee evaluation tool. It was designed as a high level organization management tool. That means that not everyone in the organization needs to have ownership of plan components. The concept of focus and critical few implies that not all effort is documented. Forcing the plan to be deployed to everyone in the organization creates a huge Hoshin plan and runs the risk of diluting focus. This is especially true if individual improvement plans become part of the organization's Hoshin plan.

Linking compensation directly to achieving Hoshin objectives can have the effect of the organization becoming risk adverse. When people know their pay will be directly impacted by the objectives they sign-up for, they tend to select small gains which they are confident will be achieved instead of high-risk objectives that might fail. The other problem of linking compensation or bonuses to Hoshin plan performance is that the objectives selected may not actually impact the desired performance. I remember a situation at HP where every lower level objective was met, but business didn't improve. The causes were that some objectives took longer to see the effect and others didn't have the contribution we expected. In that case, we would have all received bonuses when the business was going in the wrong direction.

This subject is probably better addressed in another book, but let me give you my personal opinion. I think the Hoshin plan should remain as management's tool to set organization direction and monitor organization and process performance. I don't believe the Hoshin plan can replace your current employee performance evaluation or compensation and bonus programs. I think individual performance evaluations should have a section that documents how well the individual supported the organization's plan but not much more. Individual growth objectives should not clutter the organization's Hoshin plan. Of course there is no reason why individuals can't create their own

personal growth Hoshin plan outside of the organization's plan. I personally believe that compensation and bonus should not be directly tied to the Hoshin plan. Compensation should be based on the competitive value of the job's requirements and bonuses should be based on the success of the organization. I don't pretend to be an expert in this area, but based on my experience, the most successful Hoshin Kanri implementations used Hoshin to manage the organization and didn't try to use it to manage individual employees.

Summary

Hoshin Kanri is used by many world-class organizations to focus effort on the critical few things necessary for success. Hoshin is a system of forms and rules that provides structure to the planning process. It encourages employees to analyze situations, create plans for improvement, conduct performance checks, and take appropriate action. It's a powerful communication tool and helps everyone in the organization understand how their efforts contribute to the organization's overall success. Hoshin is driven by data and not by opinions. It's founded on the principles of Management by Objectives and the PDCA improvement cycle and uses periodic reviews to assure continuous improvement.

Implementation is not easy, however. It takes management discipline to overcome the barriers and avoid common mistakes, but it is well worth the effort. Successful implementation of Hoshin Kanri helps organizations become more effective.

Notes

Chapter 8

Hoshin Planning Forms

Hoshin is primarily defined by the forms that are used to facilitate the process. There are four basic concepts used in Hoshin Planning. They are: 1) objective and key strategy deployment, 2) business fundamentals management, 3) review of progress, and 4) resolving problems. During Hoshin implementation, every organization tends to develop a specific set of forms that fits its specific situation and culture. As a result, there is no one correct set of forms.

As a starting point for the first time user, however, I have documented a set of seven forms that I found useful. The seven forms are used to document the Hoshin plan and facilitate its implementation. For the most part, the forms are the same ones I used at Hewlett-Packard back in the 1980s. Together they form what I call a "manual" process of Hoshin implementation. Recognize that back in the 1950s, when Hoshin was first documented, personal computers had not been invented. Hoshin forms were hand drawn and completed.

You don't need software to implement Hoshin. You can use the manual forms as a guide and design your own Hoshin forms. Of course, software makes the Hoshin process a whole lot easier. Since TQE's software was introduced back in 1994, I no longer use the forms described in this chapter. However, the Hoshin software was based on the forms and understanding them provides a better understanding of the Hoshin process.

PM: Performance Measures

Hoshin Planning Table

General Comments: This table is used to document and deploy key activities necessary to improve the organization's situation. It's useful for both long range planning and annual planning. Required elements of the table include: 1) a situation statement, 2) an objective for improvement and its associated PMs/deliverables (goals), and 3) one or more strategies and their associated PMs/deliverables (goals). This form can be modified slightly to document business fundamentals.

Situation: Document the environment in which the plan was generated. It should include all pertinent information necessary for one to conclude that the objective is the right thing to do at this time. It's appropriate to include world events, organization performance data, higher order goal alignment, results of last year's plan, and any other information that could influence the organization's course of action.

Objective: Describe the most important thing to be accomplished, based on the situation. It's recommended that the objective be written in "issue statement" form, i.e., includes: 1) an indicator of change, 2) the PM that will measure the change, and 3) the process to be changed.

> Examples: Improve response time of customer request for parts.
> Decrease part shortages in final product packaging.
> Eliminate errors in journal entries.

Strategy: To accomplish the objective, effort may be required in different areas and/or using multiple techniques. The Strategy section documents multiple strategies necessary to achieve the objective. Only key or critical path strategies should be documented. It's recommended that no more than five strategies be documented. The sum result of all strategies should assure achievement of the objective. One should ask, "If all of the strategies were accomplished, will the objective be achieved?" Issue statement form is also appropriate for strategies. When deployed to lower level planning tables, strategies and their associated PMs/deliverables (goals) should be copied verbatim. If strategies tend to be a series of well-understood tasks with completion dates, it's recommended that the Implementation Plan be used to document effort, instead of this form.

Owner: The person responsible for accomplishment of the objective/strategy is noted in parentheses. Avoid vague names like "team" or "all." If you find it necessary to use such terms, lower level deployment should ultimately describe a one strategy one owner relationship. The owner is the person that says, "You can count on me."

PMs/Deliverables (Goals): The performance measures (PMs) that will be monitored to track progress and the anticipated final value of the PM (goal) are documented in this section. At least one PM should be defined; specifically the one addressed in the objective/strategy statement. In addition, counter balancing PMs should also be selected with goals established for minimum acceptable levels. To determine if a counter balancing PM is required, ask yourself this question, "Is there anything I can do to optimize this PM, but I know it's the wrong thing to do?" If the answer is "Yes" then you need counter balancing PMs. If the objective/strategy is an improvement project, then the key milestones or deliverables are also documented in this section. The deliverable goal is the expected date of completion.

Hoshin Planning Table

Location:	Time Period:
Prepared By:	Date:

Situation:	

Objective, based on situation:	
Objective (Owner)	PMs/Deliverables (Goals)
0	

Key Strategies necessary to achieve Objective:	
Strategy (Owner)	PMs/Deliverables (Goals)
1	
2	
3	
4	
5	

Implementation Plan

General Comments: When accomplishment of an objective can be achieved by executing a series of well-understood tasks with completion dates, the Implementation Plan should be used to document activity, instead of using the Hoshin Planning Table. The Implementation Plan is used to document a sequence of activities or tasks with respect to time. The required elements of the form are: 1) a description of the activity/task to be accomplished, 2) task ownership assignment, 3) a description of the task deliverable, and 4) a time axis, where tasks are scheduled. Popular project management software includes all of these elements and is acceptable for use as Implementation Plans. Software may be required for complex improvement projects, but a simple Implementation Plan will probably suffice for the majority of projects.

Objective: The objective is a restatement of a strategy from the higher level Hoshin Planning Table.

Activity/Task: This column allows the objective to be broken up into small manageable portions, called activities or Tasks. Each task should be a stand alone activity that is well understood and has a desired completion date. The specific inputs necessary to begin the task should be available. The actual time to accomplish the task should be predictable with reasonable accuracy. The finished product or deliverable of the task should also be obvious. Some tasks are linked to others, and the Implementation Plan can show that linkage.

Owner: The person responsible for task accomplishment is recorded in this column. Correct use of this column allows the objective owner to assure that resources are effectively utilized. It's important to balance the work and to make appropriate use of people's talents. It's best to only have one person listed for each task. The owner may not do all the work, but you can count on them to assure the task is completed. If it's desirable to include supporting people, they can be noted in parentheses. Vague, general ownership descriptions like "team" or "all" should be avoided.

Deliverable: This column describes the finished product of a task. A deliverable is tangible evidence that a task is complete.

Examples:

Activity/Task	Deliverable
Conduct training session	Student Evaluations
Order work material	Supplies in-house
Meeting to discuss issues	Summary report distributed
Build prototype	Prototype working as expected

Calendar: This section is used to layout the tasks with respect to time. It shows the relationship of one task to others and allows the overall objective activities to be viewed. Since most planning cycles are done annually, the time frame is typically one year. For shorter projects, the scale can be changed.

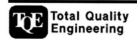

Implementation Plan

Prepared By:	Date:	Fiscal Year:	Location:	Dept:
Reviewed By:	Date:	Objective/Project:		

No.	Activity/Task	Owner	Deliverable	Q1			Q2			Q3			Q4		
				Jan	Feb	Mar	Apr	May	Jun	Jul	Aug	Sep	Oct	Nov	Dec

Total Quality Engineering

Hoshin

Periodic Review Table

General Comments: This form is used to document the periodic review process. It's recommended that review of progress occur monthly for almost all bottom level planning tables. Higher level tables may be reviewed quarterly or annually. This form should be completed by the objective owner and reviewed with the next level of management. If the Review Table Summary is used during the actual review instead of this form, it's still recommended that the objective owner use this form for backup documentation. The content of the review form is based on the Plan-Do-Check-Act (PDCA) cycle. The review process also documents changes to the plan without having to recreate it. Simply keeping track of "Expected results next period" documents plan deviations.

Objective Description and **PMs/Deliverables (Goals)**: These items should be copied verbatim from the objective and PMs/deliverables (goals) sections of the appropriate Hoshin Planning Table.

Expected results this period: Describe the deliverables and/or accomplishments that were expected to be completed during the period covered by the review. It should be as specific as possible with reference to numbers and real events. For all reviews except the initial review of an annual plan, the description should be verbatim with the description found in the "Expected results next period" section of the previous review's form.

Actual results this period: Document the actual results achieved during the period. It should be as specific as possible, with reference to numbers and real events. It's not used to make excuses for why results were not achieved.

Analysis of deviation from expected results: In the event that actual results are different from expected results, document the underlying causes for the difference. Focus should be on process issues not people or personalities. Analysis of the root cause of deviations should be completed. To discover the root cause it's helpful to ask "Why?" five times. This forces the search beneath the obvious and helps prevent identifying symptoms as causes.

Lessons learned and implications for next period: This section allows for reflection on the lessons learned during the review period. Many early reviews of an annual plan expose the fact that the plan was too aggressive or not detailed enough. As a result, the original schedule of expected results is unrealistic. Implications for the future might well include a reworking of the original plan's schedule of events.

Expected results next period: Describe the deliverables and/or accomplishments that are expected to be completed during the next review period. Expectations documented in the original plan and past review results should be integrated to develop the next period's expected results. They should be as specific as possible, with reference to numbers and real events. The description of "Expected results next period" should be copied verbatim to the "Expected results this period" section of the following review period's form.

Periodic Review Table

Obj#:	Prepared by:		Date:

Objective Description:	PMs/Deliverables (Goals)

Expected results this period:

Actual results this period:

Analysis of deviation from expected results:

Lessons learned and implications for next period:

Expected results next period:

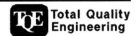

Review Table Summary

General Comments: This form is used to document the periodic review process. It's recommended that review of progress occurs monthly for almost all bottom level planning tables. Higher level tables may be reviewed quarterly or annually. The form should be completed by the objective owner and reviewed with the next level of management. The content of the review form is based on the Plan-Do-Check-Act (PDCA) cycle. The review process also documents changes to the annual plan without having to recreate it. Simply keeping track of "Expected results" for the next period, documents plan deviations.

The advantage of using the Review Table Summary instead of the Periodic Review Table is that it provides a brief status of numerous objectives on one page. The disadvantage is that there is not much room for descriptive detail. If the Review Table Summary is used during the review, it's still recommended that Periodic Review forms be used for backup documentation.

Item: Record the Hoshin activity number.

Expected Results: Describe the deliverables and/or accomplishments expected to be completed for each item during the period covered by the review. It should be as specific as possible, with reference to numbers and real events. It's appropriate to complete this column prior to the start of the review period. For example, based on the Implications for the Future described during the second quarter review, Expected Results for the third quarter would be documented on a separate form. The remainder of the form would then be completed during the third quarter review. Following this process prevents expectations from creeping between review periods.

Actual Results: Document the actual results for each item achieved during the period. It should be as specific as possible, with reference to numbers and real events. It's not used to make excuses for why results were not as expected.

Status: This column provides a quick visual indication of item status. The codes shown on the form are for example purposes. The user can customize the status codes as desired.

Analysis of Deviation: In the event that actual results are different from expected results, document the underlying causes for the difference. Focus should be on process issues, not people and/or personalities. Analysis of the root cause of deviations should be completed. To discover root cause, it's helpful to ask "Why?" five times. This forces the search beneath the obvious and helps prevent identifying symptoms as causes.

Implications for the Future: This column allows for reflection on the lessons learned during the review period. Many early reviews of the plan will expose the fact that it was too aggressive or not detailed enough. As a result, the original schedule of expected results is unrealistic. Implications for the future might include reworking of the original plan's schedule of events.

Review Table Summary

	Prepared by:	Date:		Fiscal Year:		Location/Department:
Item	Expected Results (P)	Actual Results (D)	Status	Analysis of Deviation Summary (C)		Implications for the future (A)

Status Key: ◆ Completed   ⊕ Progress   ○ Not Begun

Hoshin

Total Quality Engineering

Business Fundamentals Planning Table

General Comments: This form documents the day to day activities of the organization. It describes the activities necessary to achieve the organization's mission. Normally it only describes activities that make up 80 to 90% of the organization's efforts. There are two forms acceptable for use, each having advantages and disadvantages. This form allows documentation of the organization mission and key activities, PMs (action limits), and owners. In addition, it provides space to document the business situation upon which the mission was based.

Situation: Document the environment in which the mission and key activities were created. It's appropriate to include descriptions of the current business environment, organization customers and their needs, and any other information that provides background and insight into the mission/key activity development.

Mission: Document the primary purpose the organization exists. Typical mission statements take the form of, "*To* satisfy the needs *of* some customers *by* providing..." The "*To* satisfy the needs *of* some customers" portion of the statement fits into this section. The remainder of the typical mission statement is split up into the Key Activities section of the form.

Key Activities: Describe the key activities necessary to achieve the mission. The net effect of successful accomplishment of all key activities assures the mission will be achieved. In most cases, business fundamentals deploy along organization lines. That means there will be as many activities as there are managers/supervisors reporting to the table owner. At the lowest level of deployment, the key activities are usually the core processes of the department.

Owner: The person responsible for process management of each mission or key activity is noted in parentheses. It's recommended to not have more than one name or have vague names such as "team" or "all." One person should be held accountable for correct performance of each business fundamental activity and that owner is typically the manager/supervisor of the mission/activity.

PMs (Action Limits): For each mission and key activity, list the PMs that will be monitored to track performance and the value of the PMs that will initiate corrective action. At least one PM should be selected for each mission and key activity. In addition, counter balancing PMs should also be included. To determine if a counter balancing PM is required, ask yourself this question, "Is there anything I can do to optimize this PM, but I know it's the wrong thing to do?" If the answer is "Yes" then you need a counter balancing PM. Generic PMs for any process are Quality, Cost, Delivery, and People. Action limits are computed based on the PM's natural variability. The intent is to select an action limit that will trigger corrective action only when process variability exceeds normal levels. Do not set action limits arbitrarily or based on desired performance. It will typically require twelve to twenty data points before action limits can be accurately computed.

Business Fundamentals Planning Table

Location:		Time Period:	
Prepared By:		Date:	

Situation:

Mission, based on situation:

Mission (Owner)	PMs (Action Limits)
0	

Key Activities necessary to achieve Mission:

Activity (Owner)	PMs (Action Limits)
1	
2	
3	
4	
5	

Business Fundamentals Planning Table

General Comments: This form documents the day to day activities of the organization. It describes the activities necessary to achieve the organization's mission. Normally it only describes the activities that make up 80 to 90% of the organization's efforts. There are two forms acceptable for use, each having advantages and disadvantages. This form allows documentation of the organization mission and key strategies, PMs (action limits), and owners. Ownership can be defined to the PM level. In addition, it defines the review frequency for each PM and requires identification of the PM's data source.

Mission: Document the organization's mission and key activities necessary to achieve the mission. Typical mission statements take the form of, "*To* satisfy the needs *of* some customers *by* providing..." The "*To* satisfy the needs *of* some customers" portion of the statement fits into this block. The remainder of the typical mission statement is split up into the key activities section of the form.

Key Activities: Describe the key activities necessary to achieve the mission. The net effect of successful accomplishment of all key activities assures the mission will be achieved. In most cases, business fundamentals deploy along organization lines. That means there will be as many activities as there are managers/supervisors reporting to the table owner. At the lowest level of deployment, the key activities are usually the core processes of the department.

PM (Action Limits): For each mission and key activity, list the PMs that will be monitored to track performance and the value of the PMs that will initiate corrective action. At least one PM should be selected for each mission and key activity. In addition, counter balancing PMs should also be included. To determine if a counter balancing PM is required, ask yourself this question, "Is there anything I can do to optimize this PM, but I know it's the wrong thing to do?" If the answer is "Yes" then you need a counter balancing PM. Generic PMs for any process are Quality, Cost, Delivery, and People. Action limits are computed based on the PM's natural variability. The intent is to select an action limit that will trigger corrective action only when process variability exceeds normal levels. Do not set action limits arbitrarily or based on desired performance. It will typically require twelve to twenty data points before action limits can be accurately computed.

Reviewed: Some processes only show long term variability while others processes show high variability over the short term. The Review Period allows for tailoring how frequently a process will be reviewed. Business fundamentals are generally reviewed monthly, quarterly or annually.

Data Source: This column requires the process owner to determine from what source the PM data will be extracted. This helps prevent vague, non-measurable PMs from being selected.

Owner: The person responsible for process management of each mission and key activity is recorded in this column. It's recommended to not have more than one name or have vague names such as "team" or "all." One person should be held accountable for correct performance of each business fundamental activity. Individual ownership of each PM can also be defined.

Business Fundamentals Planning Table				page of
Prepared by:	Date:		Fiscal Year:	Location/Department:
Mission	PMs (Action Limits)	Reviewed	Data Source	Owner
Key Activities	PMs (Action Limits)	Reviewed	Data Source	Owner

Total Quality Engineering

Hoshin

Abnormality Table

General Comments: This form is used to document a deviation from normal for any process. It's typically used with respect to business fundamental PMs. Too often, problems occur over and over again. The intent of the Abnormality Table is to assure that a systematic process is followed to resolve the immediate issue and to correct the root cause of the problem so it never occurs again. The form can be modified to collect data and track problem resolution on many different types of issues, ranging from employee feedback complaints to hardware and software design problems. A count of Abnormality Tables can also be a useful PM.

Abnormality Tables are rarely completed when they are first created. The recommended approach is to complete the Abnormality Table as information becomes available. The table is created when the problem is discovered (State 3). It's updated when Root Cause is understood (State 2), when a solution is implemented (State 1), and when the solution is verified to resolve the problem (State 0). This takes the problem through the PDCA cycle. An Abnormality Table is considered "open" until the solution has been verified (State 0).

Problem Description: Document specifically what unexpected event occurred. Describe the circumstances surrounding the abnormality. Include a specific description of the abnormality, where did it occur, when did it occur, and its seriousness.

Root Cause Analysis: Document the root cause of the abnormality. Take care not to jump to solution. In fact, it's best to never propose a solution until root cause is understood. Too often what we think is a cause, is merely a symptom of the root cause. For technical problems root cause understanding can be demonstrated by turning the problem on and off at will AND being able to describe the physical mechanisms at work. For all other problems it's helpful to ask "Why?" five times. This forces the search beneath the obvious and helps prevent identifying symptoms as causes.

Solution Description: Once the root cause(s) of the problem is understood a solution can be proposed. A best practice is to not jump to the first solution. Instead, identify multiple solutions and then select the best solution using a process like decision analysis or weighted multi-voting. Once the solution is selected its implementation should be scheduled. At this point the Solution field is completed documenting the process of selecting the solution and scheduling its implementation. Avoid the tendency to assume that training will solve all problems. While training new people is essential and refresher training may help in the short run, training is not an irreversible solution. It's best to identify solutions that reduce or eliminate the need for training.

How Solution was Verified: After the solution has been fully implemented it should be verified that it completely solved the problem and didn't create any new problems. Describe the results of trials or experiments that demonstrate the solution was effective. If the abnormality caused a performance measure to exceed its action limits, then it should be verified that performance has returned to normal.

Abnormality Table

Process name:	Prepared by:	Date:

3. Problem Description:

2. Root Cause Analysis:

1. Solution Description:

0. How Solution was Verified:

Chapter 9

Hoshin Plan Examples

This chapter shows example Hoshin plans for two organizations. The first example is for a small manufacturing organization, Rockford International. Rockford wants to expand its business into international markets. The second example is for a service organization. Great Northern is an insurance company and is trying to maintain its leadership position. The Rockford example is a "manual" process utilizing the forms shown in Chapter 7. In this example, forms were created using a word processor. The Great Northern example uses Hoshin Planning software provided by Total Quality Engineering Inc. The fundamental concepts are the same in both examples, but you will also see subtle differences.

While both examples are fictitious, they are based on real experiences and attempt to show what a reasonably complete Hoshin plan might look like. By studying the examples, you should get an idea of successful Hoshin implementation. Your first efforts will probably not yield similar results so keep these examples in mind as a target for your planning process improvement.

If you have TQE's Hoshin software installed (full or free trial version), you will also find another example plan for Ridgecrest School District.

Rockford International

Rockford employs 130 people. It manufactures and sells hinges and mounting hardware to cabinetmakers. The organization chart is shown below. The example is focused on Pat Shepard, the manager of the Materials Department, and Tom Terrific, a materials engineer. Although there are many variations of how Hoshin can be applied, this example provides one complete set of forms. It includes business fundamentals, long range, and annual plans, and review tables through the first quarter review of fiscal year 2005. It also shows how abnormality tables are used to support the plan.

It's reasonable to expect a person like Pat to possess a complete set of forms, as shown in the example. Even Tom's level will sometimes have a complete set. It should be clear from the example, exactly what Pat and Tom's expectations are with respect to business fundamentals and breakthrough activities. You should also be able to follow how their specific activities link to the overall objectives of Rockford International.

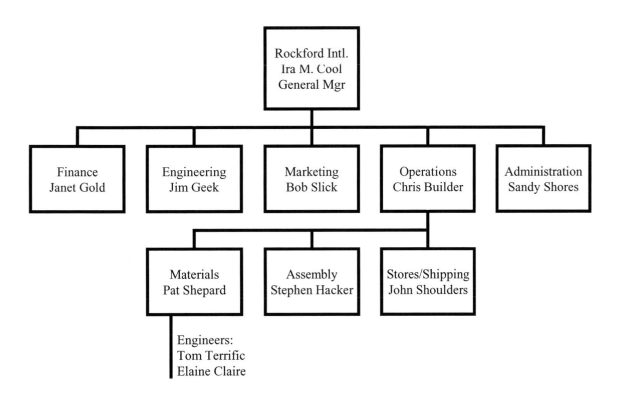

Business Fundamentals Planning Table

Location: Rockford International	**Time Period:** FY2005
Prepared By: Ira M. Cool	**Date:** 12/10/2004

Situation:

Rockford International (RI) is a small organization supplying hardware for the building industry. Rockford specializes in designing, manufacturing, and selling hinges for cabinet doors. RI employs 130 people and has revenues of $10M. Its primary customers are Southern California custom cabinetmakers. RI's business is very volatile and it's difficult to predict when their next contract will be. When they do get a contract, however, they want to move very fast and can't wait for parts. RI supports them by building and stocking a wide variety of hinges and associated fasteners. RI is capable of delivering product within one day of the order. In the rare event when product is defective, RI commits to replacing the product the same day. By virtue of excellent delivery, RI charges premium prices for its products.

Mission, based on situation:

Mission (Owner)	PMs (Action Limits)
0 Improve the responsiveness of Southern California custom cabinetmakers by providing hinges and fasteners with one day turnaround time. (Ira)	1. % orders filled same day (<95%) 2. Revenue (<$500K/mo) 3. Profit (<6%) 4. Cust Sat (<95%)

Key Activities necessary to achieve Mission:

Activity (Owner)	PMs (Action Limits)
1 Maintain Rockford International customer satisfaction by consistently shipping quality products within one day of receiving an order. (Chris)	1. Line item fill rate (<95%) 2. Inventory (>2 mo supply) 3. Product returns (>0.5%) 4. Units/assembler (<150K)
2 Manage Rockford International's revenue stream by supporting current customers and attracting new customers. (Bob)	1. Orders (<80% of forecast) 2. Order growth (<10%/yr) 3. Customer calls (>20/mo) 4. Sales cost (>10% of rev$)
3 Fuel Rockford International's growth by developing new products, and assure customer satisfaction by providing technical support for current products. (Jim)	1. # Stop ships (>0) 2. # new products introduced per year (<10) 3. R&D cost (>10% rev$)
4 Assure Rockford International's profitability by providing information so that sound business decisions can be made. (Janet)	1. Profit (<target/mo) 2. Acct receivable (>45 days) 3. Acct payable (>45 days) 4. Audit score (<95%)
5 Assure Rockford International productivity by attracting, retaining, and training exceptional people and assure employee satisfaction by providing a safe, comfortable, equitable, and professional working environment. (Sandy)	1. # voluntary terminations (>2/mo) 2. # complaints (>5/mo) 3. Lost work hours (>5%)

TQE Total Quality Engineering

Business Fundamentals Planning Table

Location: RI, Operations	Time Period: FY2005
Prepared By: Chris Builder	Date: 12/10/2004

Situation:

Rockford International (RI) is a small organization supplying hardware for the building industry. Rockford specializes in designing, manufacturing, and selling hinges for cabinet doors. RI customers expect immediate delivery of products. RI Operations is responsible for managing the resources necessary to fabricate and ship products to customers.

Mission, based on situation:

Mission (Owner)	PMs (Action Limits)
1 Maintain Rockford International customer satisfaction by consistently shipping quality products within one day of receiving an order. (Chris)	1. Product LIFR (<95%) 2. Inventory (>2 mo supply) 3. Product returns (>0.5%) 4. Units/assembler (<150K)

Key Activities necessary to achieve Mission:

Activity (Owner)	PMs (Action Limits)
1.1 Source material for fabrication of RI products and assure adequate material is on hand to meet the build plan. (Pat)	1. LIFR of production material pulls (<95%) 2. Matl discrepancy reports (>0) 3. Cost of purchased matl (>40% revenue $)
1.2 Fabricate components and assemble products for shipment to RI customers according to the build plan. (Stephen)	1. Build linearity (<90%) 2. QA rejects (>5%) 3. Labor cost (>10% revenue $)
1.3 Manage flow and storage of incoming material and finished products. (John)	1. Ave time to pull and ship order (>1 hr.) 2. Inventory accuracy (<99%) 3. Total logistics cost (>2% revenue $)

Total Quality Engineering

Hoshin Handbook

Prepared by: Pat Shepard	Date: 12/10/2004		Fiscal Year: FY2005		Location/Department: Operations-Materials
Mission	**PM (Action Limit)**	**Reviewed**	**Data Source**		**Owner**
1.1 Source material for fabrication of RI products and to assure adequate material is on hand to meet the build plan.	1. LIFR of production material pulls (<95%)	Monthly	LIFR Report		Pat Shepard
	2. Matl discrepancy reports (>5)	Daily	DR Report		Pat Shepard
	3. Cost of purchased matl (>40% revenue $)	Monthly	Accounting Statement		Pat Shepard
Key Activities	**PM (Action Limit)**	**Reviewed**	**Data Source**		**Owner**
1.1.1 Order material to support build plan.	1. Ave lead time (>4wks)	Monthly	Order Status Report		Elaine Claire
	2. Stock supply (>2wks)	Monthly	Inventory Status Report		Elaine Claire
1.1.2 Select suppliers based on TQRDC parameters.	1. # suppliers (>40)	Monthly	Order Status Report		Tom Terrific
	2. # suppliers with TQRDC < 95% (>2)	Quarterly	TQRDC data base		Pat Shepard
1.1.3 Work with suppliers to resolve current issues and prevent future occurrence.	1. # open issues (>5)	Monthly	Issue Status Report		Tom Terrific
	2. Time to close issue (>4wks)	Monthly	Issue Status Report		Tom Terrific
1.1.4 Support new product programs by serving on new product teams.	1. Hrs of team activity (<20hr/mo)	Monthly	Time Logs		Elaine Claire
	2. # improvements (TBD)	Monthly	Time Logs		Tom Terrific

Long Range Planning Table

Location: Rockford International	Time Period: FY2005 to FY2010
Prepared By: Ira M. Cool	Date: 12/10/2004

Situation:

Rockford International (RI) is a small organization supplying hardware for the building industry. Rockford specializes in designing, manufacturing, and selling hinges for cabinet doors. RI employs 130 people and has revenues of $10M. Its primary customers are Southern California cabinetmakers. RI's products tend to be priced higher than competitive products, and there have been some problems with product quality. With the economy in deep recession, new home starts are at very low levels. As a result, RI orders are at all time lows. For RI to grow, it must expand its customer base outside of Southern California. Rockford International's vision is to live up to its name by providing products to a world wide customer base.

Key Objective, based on situation:

Objective (Owner)	PMs (2010 Goals)
0 Expand Rockford International's customer base to a world wide market. (Ira)	1. # Countries where RI products are sold (>20) 2. Revenue (>$500M) 3. Profit (>8%) 4. Quality (<0.01% returns)

Key Strategies necessary to achieve Objective:

Strategy (Owner)	PMs (2010 Goals)
1 Shift marketing strategy from direct sales to high volume dealers. Expand the dealer base to non US countries, with special emphasis on Europe and Asia. (Robin)	1. Orders/customer (>$10M) 2. # Countries where RI products are sold (>20) 3. Ave Discount (<40%)
2 Improve product quality and reliability. (Jim)	1. Quality (<0.01% returns) 2. Matl costs (<30% sales $)
3 Increase manufacturing capacity in order to meet world wide demand for products. (Chris)	1. WW capacity (>500M) 2. Units/assembler (>600K) 3. Assembler annual turnover (<3%)
4 Improve quality of all day to day activities, throughout the organization. (Ira-Staff)	1. All BFPT quality PM improvement (>70%) 2. Other BFPT PM improvement (>20%) 3. Dept cost (<budget)

Total Quality Engineering

Annual Planning Table

Location: Rockford International	Time Period: FY2005
Prepared By: Ira M. Cool	Date: 12/10/2004

Situation:

For Rockford International to achieve its long range vision, it must expand its customer base beyond Southern California. Market research has shown that new home starts are growing faster in Spain than anywhere else in the world. Spanish contractors buy almost all of their supplies from one distributor, El Partes. For El Partes to distribute material, they require it be manufactured with at least 30% Spanish labor. They have a reputation for only distributing high quality parts at reasonable prices. They do, however, expect large discounts from their suppliers. The Spanish government wants to encourage business, and will provide tax breaks and other special incentives. If RI could distribute its parts through El Partes, RI revenue could triple in 2006 with double digit profit. To win the El Partes contract, RI will need to establish an assembly operation in Spain, with some locally sourced material. It will also need to improve product quality and reduce operating cost.

Key Objective, based on situation:

Objective (Owner)	PMs (Goals)
0 Establish a production facility in Barcelona Spain and have RI products distributed by El Partes. (Ira)	1. Assembly plant operational (Q3,05) 2. El Partes contract signed (Q4,05) 3. Ship first hinge (1/1/06) 4. Overall project cost (<$750K)

Key Strategies necessary to achieve Objective:

Strategy (Owner)	PMs (Goals)
1 Work with Spanish government to secure all necessary licenses and agreements. (Bob)	1. License obtained (Q1,05) 2. Apply for Spanish grant (Q2,05)
2 Begin assembly operation in Spain. (Chris)	1. Building leased (Q2,05) 2. Employees hired and trained (Q3,05) 3. Local supplier selected (Q3,05)
3 Improve the quality and reliability of the 15009 hinge family. (Jim)	1. Quality (0.1% returns) 2. MTBF (1M hrs) 3. Cost (%current cost) 4. New Prod Intro (Q4,05)
4 Improve cost structure of RI Business operations. (Ira-Staff)	1. R&D Cost (<9% rev$) 2. Sales Cost (<8% rev$) 3. Mfg Cost (<30% rev$) 4. Ovrhead Cost (<3%rev$)

Annual Planning Table

Location: RI-Operations	**Time Period:** FY2005
Prepared By: Chris Builder	**Date:** 12/10/2004

Situation:

For Rockford International to expand its market base, it needs to distribute parts in other countries. Market research has shown that the best opportunity today is in Spain. If RI could supply hinges to the fast growing, Spanish, home building industry it could significantly improve its business position. Almost all parts used by Spanish home builders are purchased through the distributor, El Partes. The requirements to supply hinges to El Partes includes having a Spanish facility, staffed with Spanish workers. In addition, 30% of the material used in assembly must be purchased in Spain. These restrictions are mandated by the Spanish Government.

Key Objective, based on situation:

Objective (Owner)	PMs (Goals)
2 Begin assembly operation in Spain. (Chris)	1. Building leased (Q2,05) 2. Employees hired and trained (Q3,05) 3. Local supplier selected (Q3,05) 4. First parts shipped (Q4,05)

Key Strategies necessary to achieve Objective:

Strategy (Owner)	PMs (Goals)
2.1 Complete all activities necessary to select site and begin production in the new Spanish Operation. (Stephen)	1. Alternatives identified (Q1,05) 2. Selection made (Q2,05) 3. Facility ready for operation (Q3,05)
2.2 Coordinate with Human Resources to define hiring criteria, and hire ten assemblers for the Spanish operation. (John)	1. Criteria defined (Q2,05) 2. # Spanish employees (10) 3. New employees trained (Q3,05)
2.3 Select Spanish source to supply slider pin and flange assembly for the 15009 hinge family. (Pat)	1. Sources identified (Q1,05) 2. Source selected (Q2,05) 3. Parts shipped to stock (Q3,05)

Total Quality Engineering

Hoshin Handbook

Implementation Plan

Prepared By: Pat Shepard	Date:12/10/04	Location: Rockford Int'l	Dept: Operations
Reviewed By: Chris Builder	Date:12/10/04	Fiscal Year: FY2005	Objective/Project: 2.3 Select Spanish source to supply slider pin and flange assy for 15009.

No.	Activity/Task	Owner	Deliverable	Q1			Q2			Q3			Q4		
				Jan	Feb	Mar	Apr	May	Jun	Jul	Aug	Sep	Oct	Nov	Dec
1	Research alternative suppliers	Tom/Elaine	Summary report	◆											
2	Mail "Interest?" letters	Tom	Letters mailed	◆											
3	Review Replies	Tom/Elaine	10 sources selected		◆										
4	Mail 15009 part requirements and Request for Bid	Tom	Letters mailed		◆										
5	Review bids and select 3 possible suppliers	Tom/Chris	3 sources selected				◆								
6	Schedule 3 site visits	Tom	Trip itinerary				◆								
7	Conduct site visits	Chris/et.al.	Trip report					◆							
8	Select 15009 Spanish supplier	Chris/Tom	1 source selected						◆						
9	Meeting to sign contract	Chris	Contract signed							◆					
10	Evaluate first article parts	Tom	Parts meet spec.									◆			

Total Quality Engineering

Hoshin

Periodic Review Form, January, 2005

Obj#: 2.3	**Prepared by:** Tom Terrific	**Date:** 2/1/2005

Objective Description: Select Spanish source to supply slider pin and flange assembly for the 15009 hinge family.	**PPM (Goal)** 1. Sources identified (Q1,05) 2. Source selected (Q2,05) 3. Parts shipped to stock (Q3,05)

Expected results this period:

Research possible suppliers capable of manufacturing the pin and hinge assemblies. Mail letters to each potential supplier to determine if they have any interest in making the parts for RI.

Actual results this period:

Research was complete. There are over 50 machine shops in the Barcelona area that are capable of supplying the parts. Letters were not mailed, however.

Analysis of deviation from expected results:

Letters were not mailed because resources were diverted to solve problem on 37508 production operation. Refer to Abnormality number AR22. This activity has not yet reached the critical point yet. Activity can remain on schedule provided letters are express mailed within one week.

Lessons learned and implications for next period:

If I haven't solved the 37508 problem by next week, Elaine will assume responsibility for mailing the letters. As a result of the mailing delay, I may not be able to select the 10 semi-finalists next month.

Expected results next period:

Mail "Interest?" letters. Review responses and determine if "Request for Bids" can be mailed.

Periodic Review Form, February, 2005

Obj#: 2.3	Prepared by: Tom Terrific	Date: 3/1/2005

Objective Description:	**PPM (Goal)**
Select Spanish source to supply slider pin and flange assembly for the 15009 hinge family.	1. Sources identified (Q1,05) 2. Source selected (Q2,05) 3. Parts shipped to stock (Q3,05)

Expected results this period:

Mail "Interest?" letters. Review responses and determine if "Request for Bids" can be mailed.

Actual results this period:

Mailed "Interest?" letters to 56 Barcelona area machine shops on 2/10/2005. As of 3/1/2005, I have received no replies.

Analysis of deviation from expected results:

Due to the late posting date of the letters, it's not unreasonable to expect no replies so far.

Lessons learned and implications for next period:

Given the long time delays for communication via mail to Spain, future activity should probably plan on increased cost for "faxing" letters.

Expected results next period:

Review replies to "Interest?" letters and fax "Request for Bid" to 10 suppliers.

Periodic Review Form, March, 2005

Obj#: 2.3	**Prepared by:** Tom Terrific	**Date:** 4/1/2005

Objective Description: Select Spanish source to supply slider pin and flange assembly for the 15009 hinge family.	**PPM (Goal)** 1. Sources identified (Q1,05) 2. Source selected (Q2,05) 3. Parts shipped to stock (Q3,05)

Expected results this period:

Review replies to "Interest?" letters and fax "Request for Bid" to 10 suppliers.

Actual results this period:

Received 48 replies to "Interest?" letter. It seems that Barcelona machine shops are hungry for business. Based on information in their replies, Request for Bids were faxed to 15 suppliers on 3/15/05.

Analysis of deviation from expected results:

NA

Lessons learned and implications for next period:

NA

Expected results next period:

Review response of "Request for Bid" faxes and schedule site visits for 3 suppliers.

Hoshin Handbook

	Business Fundamentals Review, Q1 2005				page 1 of 1
Prepared by: Pat Shepard	Date: 4/5/2005			Fiscal Year: FY2005	Location/Department: Operations-Materials
Item	PM (Action Limit) (P)	Actual Results (D)	Status	Analysis of Deviation Summary (C)	Implications for the future (A)
0.1	LIFR of production material pulls (<95%)	98%	♥	NA	NA
0.2	Matl discrepancy reports (>5)	1 DR	♥	NA	NA
0.3	Cost of purchased matl (>40% revenue $)	37%	♥	NA	NA
1.1	Ave lead time (>4wks)	3.2 wks	♥	NA	NA
1.2	Stock supply (>2wks)	1.6 wks	♥	NA	NA
2.1	# suppliers (>40)	34 suppliers	♥	NA	NA
2.2	# suppliers with TQRDC <95% (>2)	0 suppliers	♥	NA	NA
3.1	# open issues (>5)	1 open issue	♥	NA	NA
3.2	Time to close issue (>4wks)	6 wks	⊗	Difficult problem on 37508 part. See AR22	See AR22
4.1	Hrs of team activity (<20hr/mo)	25 hrs	♥	NA	NA
4.2	# improvements (TBD)	7 improvements	♥	NA	NA

Status Key: ♥ Within Limits ∅ Caution ⊗ Exceeded Limits

Hoshin

116

 Total Quality Engineering

Abnormality Report (AR22)

Process name: 37508 Production	Prepared by: Tom Terrific	Date: 1/18/2005

3. Problem Description:

On 1/18/05, the 37508 production received a new lot of hinge pins. They did not fit without filing off the ends. This slowed down assembly, but they were able to meet the daily build plan. The lot received on 1/27/05 would not fit unless filed to the point of weakening the pin. This shut down production. Later investigation showed that filed parts were prone to breaking after less than 100 cycles. 2000 parts were shipped using the filing process.

2. Root Cause Analysis:

The supplier of the 37508 pins modified the pin fabrication process in early December, 2004. A new pin material was selected for its lower cost. The new pin becomes brittle with any grinding, and therefore the "taper" step was omitted. This made insertion of the pin into the hinge assembly difficult. Filing the pins allowed them to be inserted, but it also weakened the pins.

1. Solution Description:

The supplier had a stock of old pins. These were used to startup 37508 production again on 2/10/05. Customers that were sent weakened parts were contacted and sent replacement parts. Solution requires installing a new grinder. Supplier will only use old material, until new process can be refined.

0. How Solution was Verified:

On 2/26/2005, received shipment of pins using the improved fabrication process. These pins fit well in the assembly and showed no signs of weakness on the bend force measurement. Supplier was able to reduce his cost by 30%. Our price will also be reduced by 15%.

Hoshin Handbook

		Annual Plan Summary Review, Q1 2005			page 1 of 1
	Prepared by: Chris Builder	Date: 4/5/2005		Fiscal Year: FY2005	Location/Department: RI-Operations
Item	Expected Results (P)	Actual Results (D)	Status	Analysis of Deviation Summary (C)	Implications for the future (A)
2.1	Alternatives for Spanish operation identified.	Five potential sites were selected in the Barcelona area. Decision matrix has been completed.	◆	NA	Activity is on schedule.
2.3	Identify three potential suppliers of the pin and flange parts of the 15009.	Potential supplier list has not yet been narrowed to three.	⊕	Experience delays using the mail. Took much longer than expected to communicate with Spanish suppliers.	All future communication will be conducted using fax transmissions. This has proved very effective.

Status Key: ◆ Completed   ⊕ Progress   O Not Begun

 Total Quality Engineering

	Annual Plan Summary Review, Q2 2005			page 1 of 1	
Prepared by: Chris Builder	**Date:** 7/3/2005			**Fiscal Year:** FY2005	**Location/Department:** RI-Operations
Item	**Expected Results (P)**	**Actual Results (D)**	**Status**	**Analysis of Deviation Summary (C)**	**Implications for the future (A)**
2.1	Select site of Spanish operation and sign necessary agreements.		O		
2.3	Select supplier for to pin and flange parts of the 15009.		O		

Status Key: ◆ Completed ⊕ Progress O Not Begun

 Hoshin

 Total Quality Engineering

Great Northern

Great Northern[21] (GN) provides property and casualty insurance to commercial property owners (small businesses) and residential property owners (individuals). Great Northern's product is a piece of paper and a promise that commits Great Northern to provide specified and contractual protections in the case of certain types of loss. Employing over 1500 employees, Great Northern serves customers throughout the United States and has begun to conduct business internationally. Great Northern is a leader in its industry and wants to become the "best" insurance provider.

This example centers on the Information Technology Manager, Hubert Jacobs. From the business fundamentals planning tables, you can see how Hubert and his departments support Great Northern's day to day activities. You can also see how Hubert is supporting breakthrough activities to make Great Northern the "best insurer in the insurance industry."

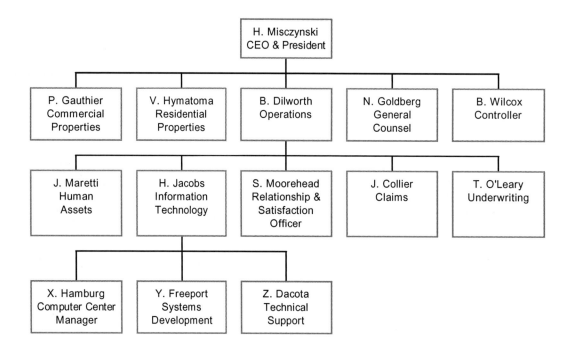

---

[21] The Great Northern example is based upon the 1994 Malcolm Baldrige National Quality Award case study that was used to prepare Examiners.

Great Northern

Business Fundamentals, 2005

Great Northern

Situation

Great Northern (GN) provides property and casualty insurance to commercial and residential property owners. GN employs over 1500 people, has over $1B in assets, and serves customers in 35 states. Customers need to have confidence that insurance providers will be there when they need them. GN provides that confidence by building long term relationships with its customers and being responsive to their customer's changing needs. GN delivers products and services in a manner that all customers feel they have gained something of significant value and would be unable to obtain from a competitor.

Number	Mission	Owner
0	Provide commercial and residential property owners with "peace of mind" that they are protected from financial loss in the event their property is damaged or destroyed.	H. Misczynski

Performance Measures

PM	LAL	Last Value	UAL	Goal
Net Profit (%)	NA	8.9	NA	12
Referrals Sales (%)	NA	84	NA	95
Turnaround (Days)	4.2	6	8.42	2
Underwriting Exp (K$)	10.7	17	26.8	8

Activities to achieve the Mission

Number	Activity	Owner
1	Develop and market products and services to meet the needs of commercial customers.	P. Gauthier
2	Develop and market products and services to meet the needs of residential customers.	V. Hymatoma
3	Provide pre and post sales support to customers to assure their satisfaction with GN.	B. Dilworth
4	Provide legal counsel to minimize litigation and loss.	N. Goldberg
5	Assure GN is able to meet financial commitments to its customers and shareholders.	F. Wilcox

Hoshin

Total Quality Engineering

Great Northern
Business Fundamentals, 2005

Great Northern

Situation

Customers must have confidence in their insurance providers. GN provides that confidence by assuring that each customer contact is a satisfactory experience. Whether customers have simple questions or complex damage claims, GN provides a prompt, courteous, and accurate response to all inquiries.

Number	Mission	Owner
3	Provide pre and post sales support to customers to assure their satisfaction with GN.	B. Dilworth

Performance Measures

PM	LAL	Last Value	UAL	Goal
Cust Sat Survey (%)	85	92	NA	100
Surplus Ratio	0.7	1.2	NA	1.5
Number Claims	NA	364	400	200
Dept Expense (K$)	90	98	110	100

Activities to achieve the Mission

Number	Activity	Owner
3.1	Assure that each Great Northern associate is performing at peak effectiveness by attracting, training, and supporting Great Northern's human assets.	J. Maretti
3.2	Quantify risks associated with policies and approve GN liability.	T. O'Leary
3.3	Process customers claims consistent with contract requirements.	J. Collier
3.4	Assure customers are satisfied with their GN relationship.	S. Moorehead
3.5	Provide Information Technology tools to improve GN's ability to serve its customers.	H. Jacobs

Great Northern
Business Fundamentals, 2005

 **Great Northern**

Situation

> For GN associates to provide exceptional customer service, they must have tools to increase the accuracy and efficiency of each customer interaction. GN is committed to using the newest technology to improve our operations and make associates' jobs more meaningful.

Number	Mission	Owner
3.5	Provide Information Technology tools to improve GN's ability to serve its customers.	H. Jacobs

Performance Measures

PM	LAL	Last Value	UAL	Goal
System Uptime (%)	95	98	NA	100
Support Calls	NA	88	100	0
Associate Fdbk	5	6.4	NA	10
Dept Expense (K$)	90	98	110	100

Activities to achieve the Mission

Number	Activity	Owner
3.5.1	Manage computer center and distributed networks to maximize system availability.	X. Hamburg
3.5.2	Research, evaluate and implement new systems consistent with GN's objectives.	Y. Freeport
3.5.3	Provide technical support to GN associates.	Z. Dacota

 Hoshin

 **Total Quality Engineering**

Hoshin Handbook

Great Northern
Performance Measures: Business Fundamentals, 2005

 Great Northern

<u>Number</u>

0

<u>Mission</u>

Provide commercial and residential property owners with "peace of mind" that they are protected from financial loss in the event their property is damaged or destroyed.

<u>Owner</u>

H. Misczynski

Net Profit (%)
+ Goal ● PM

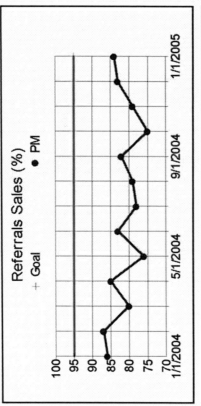

Referrals Sales (%)
+ Goal ● PM

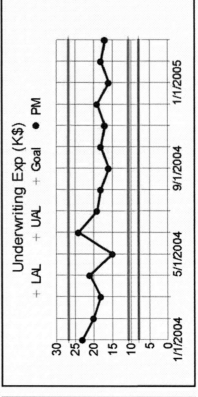

Turnaround (Days)
+ LAL + UAL + Goal ● PM

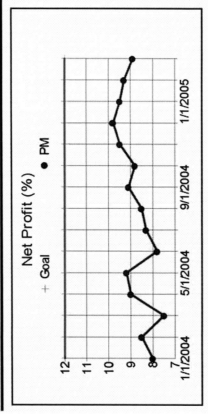

Underwriting Exp (K$)
+ LAL + UAL + Goal ● PM

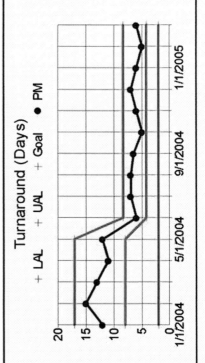

Total Quality Engineering

Hoshin

Great Northern

Long Range Plan, 2005

Great Northern

Situation

> Public frustration with the insurance industry is growing. In general, customers are dissatisfied with escalating insurance premiums, inadequate service, and changes in insurance availability. Competitors have been focusing on improving the "image" of the insurance industry, but GN believes that superior service will be the key determinate of future business success. To maintain its leadership position into the next century, GN must continue to lead the industry with innovative solutions that are delivered to customers promptly and efficiently. This will allow services to improve and maintain premiums at reasonable levels. Key success factors include diversifying GN's product base and expanding to locations throughout the world. GN's vision is to be recognized by Insurance Update as the best company in the insurance industry.

Number	Objective	Owner
0	Achieve a world-class leadership position within the insurance industry by improving customer satisfaction, employee satisfaction, and GN's ability to provide exceptional customer service.	H. Misczynski

---

Performance Measures

PM	LAL	Last Value	UAL	Goal
Cust Sat Survey (%)	85	92	NA	100
Associate Fdbk	5	6.4	NA	10
Net Income (M$)	5	6.7	NA	8
Net Profit (%)	NA	8.9	NA	12

Strategies to achieve the Objective

Number	Strategy	Owner
1	Strengthen GN's customer orientation.	S. Moorehead
2	Make GN a great place to work.	B. Dilworth
3	Enhance the quality and quantity of community involvement.	T. O'Neal
4	Implement continuous quality improvement in everything we do.	P. Gauthier
5	Improve GN's results orientation.	F. Wilcox

Great Northern
Annual Plan, 2005

 **Great Northern**

Situation

> To achieve world-class status requires world-class associates. Associate satisfaction surveys have exposed the fact that associates would like more control of their working hours. Studies of Malcolm Baldrige National Quality Award winners indicate they provide a variety of benefits and activities that improve employee empowerment and job satisfaction. The studies suggest a strong linkage between employee satisfaction and business results. For GN to achieve its vision, it must begin with improving associates' job satisfaction.

Number	Objective	Owner
0	Improve GN's associate satisfaction and strengthen associate's commitment to customers, GN and the community.	H. Misczynski

Performance Measures

PM	LAL	Last Value	UAL	Goal
Cust Sat Survey (%)	85	92	NA	100
Associate Fdbk	5	6.4	NA	10
Net Income (M$)	5	6.7	NA	8
Net Profit (%)	NA	8.9	NA	12

Strategies to achieve the Objective

Number	Strategy	Owner
1	Investigate and propose alternatives to improve associate empowerment and relationships.	S. Moorehead
2	Increase associate flexibility to determine their own work schedules and provide services to reduce associate anxiety.	B. Dilworth
3	Develop a community involvement plan.	T. O'Neal
4	Define and implement associate benefit improvements.	J. Maretti
5	Develop and implement an associate recognition tracking system.	F. Wilcox

TQE Total Quality Engineering

 Hoshin

Great Northern

Annual Plan, 2005

 **Great Northern**

Situation

For GN associates to provide exceptional customer service, they must be satisfied with their work environment. GN has historically led the industry with employee involvement and benefit programs, but associate surveys have indicated needs for a more flexible work schedule and child care. If these issues are improved, associates could devote more of their attention to customers.

Number	Objective	Owner
2	Increase associate flexibility to determine their own work schedules and provide services to reduce associate anxiety.	B. Dilworth

Deliverables of the Objective

Due	Deliverable	Owner	Complete	Comments
2/1/2005	Complete design for new child care facility	V. Hymatoma		
4/1/2005	Construction begins for new child care facility	V. Hymatoma		
4/1/2005	Propose Flextime pilot to Exec Staff	H. Jacobs		
6/1/2005	Evaluate progress of Flextime pilot	H. Jacobs		
8/1/2005	New child care facility operational	V. Hymatoma		
9/1/2005	Proposal to implement Flextime within GN	B. Dilworth		

Strategies to achieve the Objective

Number	Strategy	Owner
2.1	Pilot test Flextime and four day workweek concepts.	H. Jacobs
2.2	Upgrade on-site child care facility and programs.	V. Hymatoma

Hoshin Handbook

Great Northern
Deliverable: Annual Plan, 2005

Great Northern

Number	Objective	Owner
2.1	Pilot test Flextime and four day workweek concepts.	H. Jacobs

Deliverables of the Objective

■ Complete   ▨ Late   ▨ Future

1) Identify companies using 4 day week & flextime

2) Create associate "wish list" for new work schedule

3) Complete visits of best-in-class companies

4) Propose IT implementation to Exec Staff

5) Train associates on new process

6) Review results and correct as necessary

7) Interview associates. Identify Likes & Dislikes

8) Make proposal to Exec Staff for GN implementation

Jan 05   Mar 05   May 05   Jul 05   Sep 05   Nov 05   Jan 06

Total Quality Engineering

Hoshin

Great Northern

 **Great Northern**

Review Table: January, 2005

Number	Owner	Expected Results	Actual Results	Status	Expected Results next Period
AP 1	S. Moorehead	Research best practices and identify activities that would fit into the GN culture.	Research was completed. A wealth of different techniques were discovered. It appears that all techniques are applicable to GN	●	Develop decision criteria and evaluate different techniques to determine which two or three techniques will be proposed to senior management.
AP 2	B. Dilworth	Identify organizations using flextime and four-day work week. Define design criteria for new childcare center.	Childcare center design criteria was completed, but identification of organizations using flextime was not accomplished.	✔	Visit best-in-class organizations and understand benefits and problems with flextime. Define construction schedule for new childcare center.
AP 2.1	H. Jacobs	Identify organizations using four-day week and flextime. Create wish list for new work schedule.	The wish list was complete, but organizations using four-day week and flextime were not identified.	✖	Complete visits of best-in-class organizations.
AP 3	T. O'Neal	Create cross functional team to brainstorm alternatives to increase GN's involvement within the community.	Cross functional team was created and a list of over 100 ways GN could increase community involvement was developed.	✔	Invite community leaders to join the team. Merge community leader's input with GN's list and propose one key area to implement.
AP 4	J. Maretti	Develop survey to discover what GN associates like and dislike about the current benefits program. Review exit interviews for the past year to see if benefits was a major reason why people left GN.	Survey design is complete. Exit interviews did not show any correlation between lack of benefits and people choosing to terminate their employment.	✔	Survey associates and identify strengths and weaknesses of current benefit program.
AP 5	F. Wilcox	Design recognition tracking program.	System was designed but when the system pilot was run, associates felt the system was cumbersome and not relevant to their needs.	✖	Add recognition questions to associate benefit survey and determine how they "want to be recognized."

Status ● Exceeds Expectations ✔ Meets Expectations ✖ Behind Expectations

Hoshin

129

 Total Quality Engineering

Great Northern

Review Table: Annual Plan, 2005

Great Northern

Number	Objective	Owner
2.1	Pilot test Flextime and four day workweek concepts.	H. Jacobs

Period: January
Status: Behind Expectations

Due: 2/5/2005
Complete: 2/17/2005

Expected Results

Identify organizations using four-day week and flextime. Create wish list for new work schedule.

Actual Results

The wish list was complete, but organizations using four-day week and flextime were not identified.

Analysis of Deviations

Resources were diverted to resolve the Customer Accounting system crash. One whole week was required to resolve this problem. This left no time to support breakthrough efforts.

Future Implications

Assuming solution to prevent problem reoccurrence is effective (see Abnormality Report #2) there should be enough time to get back on schedule.

Expected Results next Period

Complete visits of best-in-class organizations.

Great Northern

Abnormality Table: Business Fundamentals, 2005

Number	Mission	Owner
3.5.1	Manage computer center and distributed networks to maximize system availability.	X. Hamburg

ID: 2   **State: 0**

Problem Description   Date Found: 1/15/2005

Customer Accounting system crashed and was out of operation for five days. Customer payments had to be processed by hand. The processing delay resulted in some customers receiving late notices.

Root Cause Description   Date Understood: 1/16/2005

Power line surge corrupted data files and caused hardware failures. After repairing hardware and installing backup data files, a bad tape drive erased data and corrupted hard drive.

Solution Description   Date Solved: 1/20/2005

Replaced bad tape drive and installed surge protectors on all computer equipment. Data was reentered by hand from paper backups. Surge protectors should prevent original problem, but from now on we will keep two backup tapes.

How Solution was Verified   Date Verified: 1/30/2005

Tested system with a surge generator. Could not make system fail even with surges of 10KV. This problem should never happen again.

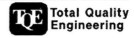

Appendix A

Hoshin Kanri and the Balanced Scorecard

In 1992 Robert S. Kaplan and David P. Norton wrote an article in the Harvard Business Review called "The Balanced Scorecard - Measures that Drive Performance." The article stressed the importance of not relying solely on financial measures to measure organizational success. It stressed the need for balance between short-term and long-term objectives, between financial and non-financial measures, between leading and lagging indicators, and between internal and external performance measures. The article was short on specific application, but its concepts struck a cord with many senior managers.

The popularity of the article forced Kaplan and Norton to write a couple of other articles in the HBR and two books on the subject (refer to the list of references in the bibliography). Each article and book attempted to provide more "how to" instructions but the majority of the content continued to focus on describing the concepts and philosophy. There are two key components of the Balanced Scorecard (BSC). The first is "what gets measured gets done." The second is that financial measures are not sufficient to manage the organization. The BSC creates a dashboard of indicators from all aspects of the organization's activities. It identifies measures from the four perspectives of financial performance, customers, internal business processes, and people growth and learning. The expectation is that when these measures are linked to the organization's strategy, people will naturally adopt appropriate behaviors to achieve the goals.

The basic concepts of the BSC are not new! The BSC is very similar to the concepts of Management by Objectives introduced by Peter Drucker back in the 1950s. The concept of balancing focus on the multiple aspects of running a successful organization has been around since people began to work together. Every leader of an organization knows that you can't treat employees poorly and expect results. You can't ignore customers and then expect them to purchase additional products and services. You can't continue to use the same processes and equipment and expect productivity gains. You can't sell products and services for less than it costs to deliver them. These are basic organizational truths! Unfortunately in their rush to increase short-term shareholder value, many senior executives have forgotten these basic concepts. The primary benefit of the BSC articles and books by Kaplan and Norton is that they have helped senior executives rediscover these basic concepts.

There are now many accounts of organizations adopting the concepts of the BSC with excellent results. There are also examples of organizations that tried to implement the BSC and failed miserably. The problem is that the successful organizations (and the consultants that helped them) claim that the BSC was the cause of their success. The organizations that failed (their consultants can't be contacted) claim that the complexity

of the BSC caused its failure. In reality neither statement is true. The concepts of the BSC are excellent. It's a great tool to identify a balanced set of measures that organizations can use to manage their efforts, but it's just one piece of the total management system. It's not a silver bullet that will cure all problems. Just like any other good process it requires management investment and nurturing for success. The biggest downside of the BSC is that while the concepts are great, actual implementation is often left to the consultant's whim.

Hoshin Kanri has always stressed the importance of selecting counter-balancing performance measures to monitor results. Generic counter-balancing measures are quality, cost, delivery, and people. Consistent with the BSC approach, measures can instead be selected from the perspectives of customers, financial, internal processes, and people growth and learning. This simple change allows the bulk of the BSC philosophy to be implemented within Hoshin. Graphs of performance measures at each level of the organization provide a dashboard that is used to quickly determine status.

In addition, Hoshin Kanri provides a ready made format to implement breakthrough plans using the concepts of the BSC. All you have to do is create long range and annual plans that have improvement objectives in each of the four BSC perspectives. Deployment follows the standard Hoshin process and can be deployed to all areas of the organization.

The one problem I have with the BSC is that it lumps all activity into one plan. That means business fundamental and breakthrough objectives are both in the same plan. You end up trying to improve everything and that often results in improving nothing. I prefer to retain the Hoshin concept of separation of business fundamentals and breakthroughs. If I'm implementing the BSC using the Hoshin format, I use the four BSC perspectives for business fundamental performance measures and my breakthrough plans are deployed using the four BSC perspectives.

The bottom line is that Hoshin and the Balanced Scorecard are perfectly compatible. You don't need to choose one over the other. The only thing to keep in mind, however, is that Hoshin is bigger than the Balanced Scorecard. You can implement the Balanced Scorecard using the concepts of Hoshin, but you can't implement Hoshin using the Balanced Scorecard.

 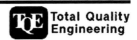

Appendix B

Hoshin Kanri and ISO 9000-2000

The International Organization for Standardization (ISO) has the mission of promoting the development of standardization and related world activities to facilitate the international exchange of goods and services. ISO is comprised of 91 member countries. The American National Standards Institute (ANSI) is the member body representing the United States. There are approximately 180 Technical Committees within ISO on a wide range of subjects. Technical Committee 176 was formed in 1979 to harmonize international activity in quality management and quality assurance standards. The ISO 9000-2000 series of standards is a result of this committee. The "2000" identifies the set of standards officially adopted in the year 2000.[22]

The ISO standards provide a framework for fundamental quality management. The standards were developed to effectively document quality system elements that should be implemented in order to maintain an efficient quality system within organizations. Organizations use accredited, independent, third party registering bodies to certify that the organization complies with the standards. Most organizations obtain registration to ISO 9001. All organizations should be capable of being registered, regardless of their decision to actually become registered. The ISO standards describe in many cases the minimal set of processes necessary for delivering quality products and services to customers. You will not win the Baldrige award by simply being registered, but if you are not registered or capable of being registered there is probably no hope that your organization will even get close to winning the Baldrige award.

ISO 9001-2000 has eight sections that auditors use to assess an organization's quality management system. Sections 4 through 8 are the "Requirements" portion of the standard.

1. Introduction
2. Scope
3. Terms and definitions
4. Quality management system
5. Management responsibility
6. Resource management
7. Product realization
8. Measurement, analysis and improvement

---

[22] For more information on the ISO 9000-2000 standards and to purchase your copy, please visit the American Society for Quality's website (http://www.asq.org).

Hoshin Kanri directly addresses the section on Management Responsibility. The standard requires organizations to provide evidence of top management's commitment to the development and implementation of the quality management system. It requires that customer input drive the planning process. It requires that the organization's quality policy be communicated to everyone. It requires that quality improvement objectives be measurable. It requires that responsibilities and authorities be clearly defined. It requires top management to check on progress and take action as necessary.

Any organization that has implemented the Hoshin Kanri planning process will have an easy time providing evidence to an auditor that the requirements of ISO 9000-2000 section 5 are being met. After referencing the Hoshin plan in their Quality Manual, they will only need to open the Hoshin plan to show that the organization's quality policy is clearly defined and communicated to everyone. Management responsibilities will be clearly identified by planning table owners. It will be obvious that all improvement activities link to the organization's quality objectives and that they are measurable. A rigorous set of review tables will clearly show management's commitment and involvement in managing the organization's quality policy. In addition, Hoshin Kanri addresses the Corrective Action clause of section 8 of the standard. Hoshin's abnormality tables provides a link between corrective action and specific core processes and helps assure that problems are solved using the systematic PDCA cycle.

Implementing Hoshin Kanri can be an excellent first step toward becoming fully compliant with ISO 9000-2000.

Appendix C

Hoshin Kanri and Six Sigma

Six Sigma methods have their roots in Motorola's quality improvement effort in the late 1980s. That effort was a major contributor to Motorola being one of the first Malcolm Baldrige winners in 1988. In the 1990s, Six Sigma achieved popular appeal as a result of the success General Electric and Allied Signal had using Six Sigma concepts.

While the name "Six Sigma" has taken on a broader meaning, the fundamental premise of Six Sigma is to improve processes such that there are at least six standard deviations between the worst case specification limit and the mean of process variation. For those of us that are statistically challenged, that means the process is essentially defect free!

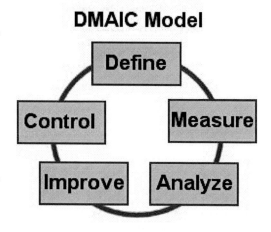

The tools of Six Sigma are not new. Most of them are the same basic tools used by Quality Improvement Teams in the 1970s and early 1980s. Six Sigma does have a catchy name and titles like "Black Belts," but its real value is in the systematic approach to improvement. The DMAIC process is a variation of PDCA that many people find helpful. There is no doubt about it; Six Sigma can help organizations improve processes.

On the other hand, many Six Sigma program managers complain that projects are all over the map. How can they make sure people are "working on the right things?" The best approach is to align Six Sigma projects with the organization's strategic business plan.

Of course aligning and focusing improvement effort on key objectives is what Hoshin Kanri is all about. In almost all cases, at the end of every branch of the annual plan is an improvement project. There is no reason why that project can't be a Six Sigma improvement project with the project deliverables based on the DMAIC model.

Forcing the bulk of all Six Sigma projects to be managed through the Hoshin plan assures that the right projects are being selected and provides visibility of progress in real time. Hoshin Kanri helps align Six Sigma projects with the organization's strategic direction.

Appendix D

Hoshin Planning Software

You don't need software to implement Hoshin Kanri. When Hoshin was first documented back in 1965, the personal computer (PC) was still a dream. People created their own hand drawn forms and manually edited them. When PCs became popular in the 1980s, Hoshin users began to create their forms using word processing or drawing software. The forms shown in Chapter 7 were created by me using MS Word back

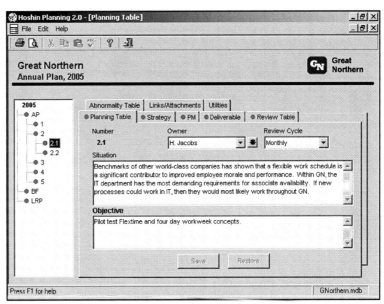

in 1992. You can create an effective Hoshin process by just using those forms and manually completing them.

Anyone that has implemented Hoshin using a manual process, however, would love to have the process automated. The biggest complaint of new Hoshin users is too much paperwork. TQE provides both PC and web-based software solutions to remove much of the overhead associated with developing and managing Hoshin plans. The software provides the plan structure and allows you to focus on the plan content. Visit TQE's web site and download the free trial software. See for yourself how it can help your organization achieve **excellence in execution**.

http://www.tqe.com

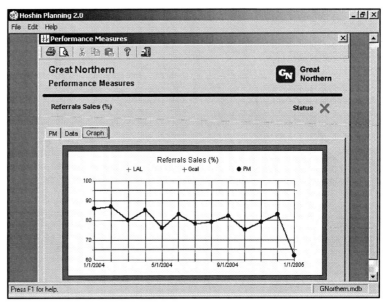

Appendix E

Measuring Hoshin Maturity

To effectively implement Hoshin Kanri, you need a measure of how well the concepts have been adopted and deployed throughout the organization. One approach is to perform periodic assessments, either by trained auditors or a "Hoshin Master." Self-assessments are effective in deploying the concepts quickly, but assessments by a Hoshin Master will provide more in depth understanding of deployment. To perform an assessment, however, you must have a set of criteria to evaluate.

The criteria described here is the criteria I typically use. I always modify the criteria to better fit the desired behaviors of the organization, but the criteria should provide you with a good starting point.

Instructions:

1. Section I is completed by senior management.

2. Section II is based on the number of business fundamental table owners. Completing item I.2 will establish the number of BFPTs and table owners. Since some people will have ownership for more than one table, their maturity score is averaged over all of their BFPTs. The section score is averaged for all table owners.

3. Section III is based on the number of tables in the annual plan. Completing item I.6 will establish the number of tables. The section score is averaged over all tables in the annual plan regardless of whether or not a person has ownership for multiple tables.

4. Maturity should be measured monthly or quarterly and a graph of the total score created.

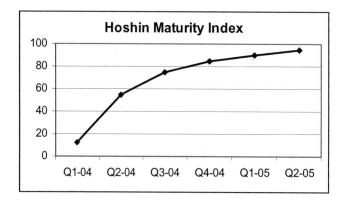

Hoshin Maturity Criteria

I. Organization Level (20 points)

1. Organization Mission defined – 2 pts
2. BFPT structure defined – 4 pts
3. Organization vision defined – 2 pts
4. LRP complete – 2 pts
5. AP key objectives defined – 2 pts
6. AP structure defined – 4 pts
7. Annual review complete – 2 pts
8. Hoshin plan for the following year complete – 2 pts

II. Business Fundamentals (per Table Owner) (40 points total)

1. Mission/Owner/Situation/Review Cycle defined – 4 pts
   a. Simple mission that is easy to remember and captures the core essence of the organization.
   b. One person identified that can be counted upon to support the mission.
   c. Situation statement contains all relevant information to justify the existence of the mission.
   d. Review Cycle is established.
2. Measures/Deliverables defined – 4 pts
   a. At least two measures (unless table is entirely managed using deliverables).
   b. Measures are balanced in the areas of quality, cost, delivery, and people.
   c. If deliverables are used, at least one deliverable is scheduled per review period.
3. Activities defined – 4 pts
   a. Typically follows organization chart.
   b. Often already defined by I-2 above.
   c. At the lowest level, activities describe department core processes or in some cases are omitted altogether.
4. BFPT catchballed with stakeholders – 4 pts
   a. Catchballed with owner of parent table.
   b. Catchballed with owners of peer tables.
   c. Catchballed with owners of lower level activities.
5. First review completed – 4 pts
6. All performance measures have data (two or more points) – 4 pts
7. Third review completed – 4 pts
8. Measures have computed action limits – 4 pts
9. Abnormality Tables used to resolve unexpected problems – 4 pts
10. BFPT is stable and capable – 4 pts
    a. Table is operating normally and as expected.
    b. Table can be reviewed by simply flashing the performance measure graphs.

Hoshin Handbook

III. Annual Plan (per Planning Table) (40 points total)

1. Objective/Owner/Situation/Review Cycle defined – 4 pts
   a. Objective identifies the key process to be improved and by how much.
   b. One person is identified that can be counted upon to assure the objective is achieved.
   c. Situation statement contains all relevant information to justify why it's important to achieve the objective.
   d. Review Cycle is established.
2. Measures/Deliverables/Goals defined – 4 pts
   a. Measures are typically used on higher order tables. They are often the same measures used for BFs. The intent is to show before and after performance.
   b. Deliverables are typically used for lower level tables. The intent is to track implementation of an improvement project that should have a positive impact on higher table measures.
   c. Performance measures goals are not limited to process capability. It's understood that improvement must be implemented before goal performance can be achieved.
   d. The goal for a deliverable is just the date due of the deliverable.
3. Strategies defined – 4 pts
   a. Deployment continues until the objective can be described as completing a series of well understood tasks or deliverables.
   b. Table strategies may have been already defined in step I-6.
4. PT catchballed with stakeholders – 4 pts
   a. Catchballed with owner of parent table.
   b. Catchballed with owners of peer tables.
   c. Catchballed with owners of lower level activities.
   d. Catchballed with all customers/users of any new process.
5. First review complete – 4 pts
6. Second review complete – 4 pts
7. Third review complete – 4 pts
8. Objective is complete – 4 pts
9. Improvements are standardized into business fundamentals – 4 pts
   a. Business fundamentals are updated as required.
   b. New measure action limits are computed.
   c. All required people trained on the new process.
10. Annual review complete – 4 pts

Appendix F

Development of Department Values
Process Description

Values: A set of deeply held beliefs and concepts that are *never* intentionally compromised.

Process Overview: Values should be developed in a meeting of everyone in the work group. The intent is to develop Values that are shared by all. If someone can't accept a word, phrase or sentence, then discussion should continue until the result is acceptable to everyone. Under no circumstances, should majority rule be imposed to obtain closure.

1. Brainstorm a list of key words and/or two word phrases that identify the key areas your Values will focus upon, (for example: Customers, People, Business Success, Leadership, Management ...)

2. Use N/3 voting to reduce the list to four key areas of focus. (Four is a suggested number. It's not a hard rule. Fewer than four could cause loss of balance and more than four runs the risk of overlap and dilution of focus.)

3. For each key area, brainstorm a list of key words and/or two word phrases that identify success factors, (for example: Customers: Satisfaction, Support, Responsiveness.)

4. Use N/3 voting to reduce each list to three success factors. (Three is a suggested number.)

5. For each success factor of each key area, obtain consensus on one sentence that captures the feel, emotion, and intent of how employees will operate to fulfill its obligations. For example:

   Expense Control: "We manage within our budget."
   Meeting Schedules: "We promise what we can deliver and deliver
     what we promise."

6. Document above results, distribute to all employees, and prominently post in the work area.

Values Example:

Operating Values[23]:

Customer Satisfaction

Customer driven: "Everything we do is driven by customer needs."
Meeting schedules: "We promise what we can deliver and deliver what we promise."
Active involvement: "We actively stay aware of our customer's activities and the external environment to prevent unsatisfactory surprises."

Expertise and Leadership

Recognized authority: "Our customers seek us out as their first choice for support."
Respected professionals: "We perform our duties with the highest standards of integrity, ethics and professionalism."
Visionary innovators: "We are constantly searching for new and innovative ways to improve our customer's success and our own performance."

People contribution

Technical competence: "We strive to know more about our area of expertise than anyone else on site."
Employee development: "Through both formal and on the job training, we continually enhance our skills, to keep pace with the changing business and technical environment."
Teamwork: "Our customers view us as an extension of their team. Within the function, we support each other and strive for synergy."

Financial performance

Expense control: "We manage within our budget."
Value added: "Our customers are better off for having used our services."
Best buy: "We provide services of higher quality and at a cost lower than any outside, competitive alternative."

5/22/1991

---

[23] This set of Values was developed by the Quality Function at the San Diego Division of Hewlett-Packard. Twelve managers developed the Values, and it was approved and accepted by the other 125 people within the function.

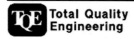 Total Quality Engineering

 Hoshin

Bibliography

Akao, Yoji, Editor: <u>Hoshin Kanri, Policy Deployment for Successful TQM</u>, Productivity Press, Cambridge, MA, 1991.

Bechtell, Michele L., <u>The Management Compass, Steering the Corporation Using Hoshin Planning</u>, American Management Association, New York, NY, 1995.

Bennis, Warren & Burt Nanus, <u>Leaders, The Strategies for Taking Charge</u>, Harper & Row, New York, NY, 1985.

Cowley, Michael & Ellen Domb, <u>Beyond Strategic Vision</u>, Butterworth Heinemann, 1997.

Deming, W. Edwards, <u>Out of the Crisis</u>, Massachusetts Institute of Technology, Cambridge, MA, 1986.

Donnelly, James H., et. al.: <u>Fundamentals of Management, Sixth Edition</u>, Business Publications, Inc., Plano, TX, 1987.

Drucker, Peter F.: <u>Management: Tasks, Responsibilities, Practices</u>, Harper & Row, New York, NY, 1974.

Drucker, Peter F.: <u>The Practice of Management</u>, Harper & Row, New York, NY, 1982.

Fallon, William K., Editor: <u>AMA Management Handbook</u>, AMACOM, New York, NY, 1983.

Hadamitzky, Wolfgang and Mark Spahn, <u>Kanji & Kana</u>, Charles E. Tuttle Organization, Tokyo, Japan, 1987.

Imai, Masaaki: <u>Kaizen</u>, Random House, Inc., New York, NY, 1986.

Ishikawa, Kaoru: <u>Guide to Quality Control</u>, Asian Productivity Organization, Tokyo, Japan, 1982.

Ishikawa, Kaoru: <u>What is Total Quality Control?</u> Asian Productivity Organization, Tokyo, Japan, 1982.

Kaplan, Robert S. & David P. Norton, <u>The Balanced Scorecard</u>, Harvard Business School Publishing Corp., 1996.

Kaplan, Robert S. & David P. Norton, <u>The Strategy Focused Organization</u>, Harvard Business School Publishing Corp., 2001.

King, Bob: <u>Hoshin Planning, The Developmental Approach</u>, Goal/QPC, Methuen, MA, 1989.

Kouzes, James M. and Barry Z. Posner, <u>The Leadership Challenge</u>, Jossey-Bass, San Francisco, CA, 1989.

Mizuno, Shigeru: <u>Organization-wide Total Quality Control</u>, Asian Productivity Organization, Tokyo, Japan, 1988.

Steiner, George A.: <u>Strategic Planning</u>, Macmillan Publishing Co., New York, NY, 1979.

Takahashi, M.: <u>Romanized Japanese-English Dictionary</u>, Charles E. Tuttle Organization, Tokyo, Japan, 1953.

Walton, Mary: <u>The Deming Management Method</u>, The Putnam Publishing Group, New York, NY, 1986.